Conduct disorder in older children and young people: research messages for practice problems

by Carol Joughin and Dinah Morley

research **in** practice

w w w . r i p . o r g . u k

Every Partner in the **research** in **practice** network receives a bulk allocation of free copies of this research review at the time of publication. Additional copies may be purchased at half price. See page 100 for purchasing information. The text is also available on our website: **www.rip.org.uk**

Published 2007
ISBN 978-1-904984-14-6

Other titles in the series:

8 *Professionalism, Partnership and Joined-up Thinking:*
 A research review of front-line working with children and families
 Nick Frost, 2005

7 *Parental Mental Health Problems: Messages from research, policy and practice*
 Jo Tunnard, 2004

6 *Disabled Parents: Examining research assumptions*
 Richard Olsen and Michele Wates, 2003

5 *Parental Drug Misuse: A review of impact and intervention studies*
 Jo Tunnard, 2002

4 *Parental Problem Drinking and its Impact on Children*
 Jo Tunnard, 2002

3 *Commissioning and Managing External Research:*
 A guide for child care agencies
 Jo Tunnard, 2001

2 *Children and Domestic Violence: A research overview of the impact on children*
 Catherine Humphreys and Audrey Mullender, 2000

1 *The Education of Children in Need: A research review*
 Ruth Sinclair, 1998

about this research review

research in **practice** aims to make it easier for those who deliver services to children and families – whether they work in local authorities, voluntary organisations, health settings or national government organisations – to access reliable research, distilled and translated with their particular needs in mind. This series of research reviews covers key practice areas identified by practitioners and key research strategy issues identified by planners and policy makers.

Challenging behaviour in children and young people frequently arises as a topic of concern and is an area of immediate importance in the government's Social Exclusion Action Plan. This topic also covers a wide and varied range of issues. So **research** in **practice** asked practitioners and policy makers in its network of more than 100 participating agencies in England and Wales which groups of children and what types of behaviour were most challenging and relevant to their practice now and what outcomes they most sought.

While answers were wide-ranging, older children and young people emerged as a group of particular concern to practitioners across disciplines. Repetitive and persistent behavioural problems in older children and young people, who meet the criteria for a diagnosis of conduct disorder*, pose challenges for professionals in children's services, health, education and a variety of fields, all of whom share an interest in improving prospects for the youths themselves and for the other people in their lives.

*'conduct disorder'
This review focuses on management issues for older children and young people who have repetitive and persistent behavioural problems that meet the criteria to enable a diagnosis of conduct disorder. Diagnosis in the UK (and the rest of Europe) is guided by the World Health Organisation's (WHO) International Classification of Diseases, 10th edition (ICD 10) (O7).

In this ninth in the **research** in **practice** research review series, two highly respected consultants and researchers with backgrounds in health and children's services join forces to help practitioners consider a range of factors that can affect outcomes for older children and young people. Addressing, in particular, ten of the most frequently asked questions arising through the **research** in **practice** network, they offer practitioners and policy makers a descriptive review of the findings of a number of relevant research reviews, along with further reading, practice examples and pointers to ongoing studies that may provide more answers in the near future.

QUALITY MARK This review has been peer-reviewed by a range of academics based in universities and service agencies, and by practitioners and others seeking to assist the development of evidence-informed practice. We are grateful for the generosity and wisdom of: Sue Bailey, Jane Barlow, Patrick Bentley, Ann Buchanan, Ann Hagell, Neal Hazel, Deborah Loeb, Helen Myatt, Rose O'Grady, Emma Poole and Michelle Sancho. The authors would also like to thank Lesley Richardson at **research** in **practice**.

Celia Atherton
Director of **research** in **practice**

about referencing

References are grouped at the back of the review according to the nature of the source material, as well as in a more traditional alphabetical listing by author. In this review the references are classified into the following categories:

A Secondary research or reviews
B Primary research or evaluations conducted in the UK
C Primary research or evaluations conducted outside the UK
D Policy and official publications
O Other sources

Citations in the text are by category as above. **research** in **practice** has adopted this method as a quick way for readers to identify the type of evidence and to find references with minimal disruption to the flow of the text.

contents

introduction

Many thousands of articles and books have been written about children and young people with challenging behaviour in disciplines as varied as molecular genetics, social anthropology, education, social work, criminology, psychology and psychiatry. It would be an impossible task to review them all systematically or to cover all the initiatives that are taking place to address the needs of these children and young people.

To offer a strong starting point for practitioners working with older children and young people (over ten years of age), this review draws on some of the key existing reviews of research in this area, focusing on children and young people with challenging behaviours who health professionals may diagnose as having conduct disorder.

For the front-line practitioner it can be very difficult to know when it might be appropriate to refer a very challenging young person for specialist help, ie, when the young person meets the criteria. We may be asking ourselves 'is this young person 'mad' or 'bad'?' Whatever we decide, the young person in question is almost certainly going to require support in a number of areas over a period of time, prompting much professional debate about who should be responsible for him or her.

> '...disturbances of mood, conduct and emerging personality are not only grey areas, phenomenologically, but hotly disputed all the way from the family through the referring agents to potential helpers, and by experienced theoreticians and practitioners too.'
> Derek Steinberg, formerly Consultant Child and Adolescent Psychiatrist, Bethlem Royal and Maudsley Hospitals, London

Our explanations for these challenging behaviours have been significantly influenced by attachment theory and, in recent years, our growing understanding of the developing brain. Studies of the infant brain suggest that the young brain 'wires up' in response to the external environment and that an enduring pattern is set in place in terms of the ways the individual responds to external stimuli. These studies bring nature and nurture together, showing how one affects the other, rather than being two parallel forces that often have been used separately to explain challenging and disordered behaviour.

Until recently it was thought that the structure and make-up of the human brain was largely fixed from early childhood onwards. However, research on post-mortem human brains and use of MRI scanning technology have demonstrated that the human brain does in fact undergo changes after this early sensitive period, and develops throughout adolescence, young adulthood and even beyond. This makes adolescence and young adulthood a time of great potential for change and development – rather than, as it was previously portrayed, a time by which character and motivation are largely fixed.

• further reading

Blakemore S-J & Frith, U (2005) *The Learning Brain: lessons for education.* Maldon MA, Oxford, Victoria (Aus.): Blackwell.

Blakemore S-J and Choudhury S (2006) 'Brain development during puberty: State of the science'. *Developmental Science* 9 (1)

Blakemore S-J and Choudhury S (2005) 'Development of the adolescent brain: Implications for executive function and social cognitition'. *Journal of Child Psychology and Psychiatry* 47

Balbernie, R (2001) 'Circuits and Circumstances: The neurobiological consequences of early relationship experiences and how they shape later behaviour'. *Journal of Child Psychology* 27 (3)

This review provides a brief description of what is meant specifically by conduct disorder, the possible causes and a short summary of the evidence to support treatment options for older children and young people. It then attempts to respond to questions that have been sent in by practitioners in the **research** in **practice** network. The focus is the management of older children and young people who already have conduct disorder. Issues relating to the prevention of conduct disorder and interventions for younger children are not specifically addressed in this review, although some examples are included and further reading is suggested in the relevant sections.

A few other resources produced by **research** in **practice** are particularly relevant to this review: Quality Protects Research Briefing 8 on *Understanding and Challenging Youth Offending*; audio series 4 discussing *Antisocial Behaviour in Young People*; Champions for Children 5 Research Briefings for Councillors on *School inclusion for all children* and, for the question of multidisciplinary working, research review 8 on *Professionalism, Partnership and Joined-up Thinking: A research review of front-line working with children and families*. There is an inevitable overlap between these resources but it is hoped that they complement each other in their content and format.

Examples of practice are inserted at various points in the text. These are mainly of services that have been positively evaluated, although a caution must be given that very often projects in one area do not transpose perfectly into another, where very different features may exist. However, they show the types of services that have been developed to respond to some of the challenges this group of young people presents and, as such, may inspire the development of projects elsewhere. Some of the examples are Child and Adolescent Mental Health (CAMHS) Innovation projects, details of which can be accessed on the YoungMinds website at:
www.youngminds.org.uk/innovationprojects

Others are from the Case Studies Database of the National Service Framework for Children, Young People and Maternity Services at:
www.childrensnsfcasestudies.dh.gov.uk/children/nsfcasestudies.nsf

and others from the National Institute for Mental Health (England) (NIMHE) – now part of the Care Services Improvement Partnership (CSIP) – Positive Practice Awards which can be found at: www.camhs.org.uk

Also inserted at various points in the text are suggestions for further reading on particular topics and flags to relevant research of particular interest that is ongoing at the time of writing, but is worth following, because, when complete, it may shed more light on some of the questions raised here.

methods

Conduct disorder is a large subject and a vast array of material is available to inform practice in this area. The research covered here has been through a variety of review processes, each of which leads to different levels of confidence about the findings and their transferability. Readers are encouraged to return to the research cited in this review for details of individual programmes.

In order to provide as much information as possible, and to complement the findings from recent research reviews, a broad search has been conducted on the websites listed below, using key words such as behavioural problems, conduct disorder, challenging behaviour, placement stability and school exclusion.

collections of systematic reviews
- Cochrane Library
- Campbell Collaboration
- Evidence for Policy and Practice Information and Co-ordinating Centre
- Auseinet

overviews of systematic reviews and primary evidence
- National Children's Bureau
- YoungMinds
- Barnardo's
- Joseph Rowntree Foundation
- Best Evidence (via Netting the Evidence)

evidence-based guidelines
- National Institute for Health and Clinical Excellence (NICE)
- Social Care Institute for Clinical Excellence (SCIE)

gateways and indexes to effectiveness resources
- National Electronic Library for Health
- Turning Research into Practice (TRIP)

other
- Office for Standards in Education (OFSTED)

- Department for Education and Skills (DfES)
- Home Office

limitations of the research

The findings of research regarding interventions for children and young people with conduct disorder should sometimes be treated with caution for the following reasons:

- Research is rarely conducted in routine settings, but under non-routine and often sub-optimal research conditions.
- Evaluations of psychosocial interventions have seldom looked for evidence of harm.
- When comparing programmes, those subject to most research will necessarily have the strongest evidence of their effects.
- Comparisons between studies are hampered by overlapping or unclear definitions or the use of incomparable outcomes.
- The majority of research has been conducted in the USA and practice may not transfer to a UK setting.
- The majority of research in this field has been conducted on boys and young men. It should not be assumed that girls and young women will respond to interventions in exactly the same way or that the outcomes would be the same.
- Research rarely addresses long-term outcomes of interventions.

what is meant by conduct disorder?

All children behave badly from time to time and occasional outbursts of temper, aggression and defiance of authority are a normal part of growing up. This review addresses management issues for older children and young people who have repetitive and persistent behavioural problems that meet the criteria to enable a diagnosis of conduct disorder to be made.

Diagnosis of conduct disorder is guided by classification systems. In the UK (and the rest of Europe) the World Health Organisation's (WHO) International Classification of Diseases, 10th edition (ICD 10) (O7) is used:

> Conduct disorders are characterised by a repetitive and persistent pattern of dissocial, aggressive or defiant conduct. Such behaviour should amount to major violations of age-appropriate social expectations. It should therefore be more severe than ordinary childish mischief or adolescent rebelliousness and should imply an enduring pattern of behaviour (six months or longer). Features of conduct disorder can also be symptomatic of other psychiatric conditions, in which case the underlying diagnosis should be preferred.

> Examples of the behaviours on which the diagnosis is based include excessive levels of fighting or bullying, cruelty to other people or animals, severe destructiveness to property, fire-setting, stealing, repeated lying, truancy from school and running away from home, unusually frequent and severe temper tantrums, and disobedience. Any one of these behaviours, if marked, is sufficient for the diagnosis, but isolated dissocial acts are not.

A full description of these diagnostic criteria can be found on the website of the World Health Organisation at: www3.who.int/icd/currentversion/fr.icd.htm (F91 deals with conduct disorder).

Professionals in the USA use the American Psychiatric Association's Diagnostic and Statistical Manual of Mental Disorders, 1994 (DSM IV) (O1), which describes three broad categories of disturbed conduct: attention deficit hyperactivity disorders (which are not specifically addressed in this review), conduct disorder and oppositional defiant disorder (ODD). ODD describes children who have marked irritability, temper outbursts, disobedience and negativity. Both ODD and conduct disorder are recognised to be heterogeneous categories and children with ODD frequently go on to develop conduct disorder and severe antisocial behaviour.

In the UK, children with conduct disorder within school settings may be classified as experiencing Emotional and Behavioural Difficulties (EBD) and may be registered as having a special educational need. The definition of EBD relies on descriptive assessments and the recognition rate of EBD is known to vary between schools. The term EBD is a broad label which has been used to group a range of difficulties such as behaviour that interferes with a child's own learning or the learning of their peers, signs of emotional turbulence and difficulties in forming and maintaining relationships. Definitions of EBD are sometimes contested and the role that societal, family and school environments play in creating and ameliorating children's social, emotional and behavioural problems must be considered.

These children will also be known to social work practitioners among the children who are looked after and children assessed as being in need.

Children and young people with conduct disorder frequently also have to contend with other problems, including attention deficit hyperactivity disorder (ADHD), impulsivity, substance abuse and depression. About half of the children with conduct disorder also have an internalising disorder such as anxiety or depression. Children with conduct disorder and co-morbid depression are at a higher risk of suicide than children with depression alone and they are more likely to harm themselves, as the young person described on the next page exemplifies.

John's story

John is an intelligent teenager who is failing to reach his potential through multiple school changes and exclusions. His behaviour has become more and more challenging as he gets older and he is involved in petty crime and substance abuse.

No school is prepared to take him because of his reputation for violent actions in the playground and sometimes in the classroom. He is less and less prepared to engage with any services and is exhibiting signs of clinical depression, ie, long periods spent alone in his room, disinterest in friends and activities. His mother cannot cope with him and he has been looked after in multiple placements over the past four years. His mother has visiting rights but does not visit. His father refuses to engage with social services in order to see his son.

When we explore John's history we find that John's parents separated shortly after his birth and are both extremely needy individuals, unable to give John the love and care he needed as a baby and the support and commitment he needs now. Both John's parents had periods in care as young people and did not have 'good enough' parenting themselves. As John's parents distanced themselves, so his behaviour became more defiant and oppositional.

The term conduct disorder is used to describe a syndrome of core symptoms, which are characterised by a persistent failure to control behaviour appropriately within socially defined rules. It has three key components: defiance of the will of someone in authority, aggressiveness, and a serious level of antisocial behaviour that violates other people's rights, property or person. Aggression and excessive disobedience in relation to adults are its key precursors (A2).

Conduct disorder is a complex interaction of the child, the environment and the context in which the child is living. Altering any of these can affect the presentation of conduct disorder. Whether interventions to address such behaviour should be medical, social, moral or legalistic is frequently debated. Professional opinion about assertive health interventions in this area is mixed. Some argue strongly that children and young people with conduct disorder are disruptive, aggressive and antisocial and that these problems require social, educational and moral solutions (O3). Others view severe conduct disorder as a chronic long-lasting illness that requires continuous monitoring and support over the life-course (A25). Questions and debate continue regarding the relationship between the family and state in the control of children who behave badly, the development of personal responsibility and about which agencies are appropriate to provide services for these children and young people. It is outside the scope of this review to consider these issues further but one review of the literature that provides a comprehensive and thoughtful consideration of these issues is Conduct Disorders in Childhood and Adolescence (A23).

Another approach to classification is to conceptualise these behaviours as being distributed along a continuum of 'overt' and 'covert' behaviours (A31). A second dimension distinguishes non-destructive from destructive behaviours. These dimensions are used to derive four subtypes of behaviour as outlined in the table below. It has been suggested that overt and covert conduct problems may represent distinct pathways to conduct disorder and delinquency, although more is known about overt than about covert conduct. Stealing represents a considerable risk for adolescent delinquency, particularly when combined with social aggression. Lying is highly correlated with stealing but appears earlier and the association becomes stronger with age (A18).

A dimensional system for classifying conduct problem behaviours

		OVERT	COVERT
NONDESTRUCTIVE		oppositional behaviour temper defiance stubborness	status violations truancy runaways
DESTRUCTIVE		aggression bullying cruelty blaming others	property violations stealing firesetting vandalism

Conduct disorder is the most common mental health disorder of childhood and its prevalence is thought to be rising (A47, B11). Practitioners are frequently reluctant to label young people with conduct disorder as having a 'mental' disorder. While this is understandable, such reluctance can result in the young person not getting the help and support s/he needs at an early stage. Children with conduct disorder often do not receive the mental health services they need in a timely manner, being frequently labelled as difficult and 'bad' and eliciting only a punitive response to their behaviours. As we have seen, whether or not children with conduct disorder should be seeking help from mental health professionals has been a controversial issue. Policy, however, now clearly identifies a requirement to address the needs of these children and young people through joined-up service provision, including contributions from professionals from health, social care and education (D7).

Readers will also be aware of government policy on antisocial behaviour, *Give Respect, Get Respect* (D10), where there is a recognition of these complex interactions and an attempt to balance punishment and support.

Persistent, poorly controlled conduct disorder has been shown to occur in 5.8 per cent of all children and young people in Britain (B27). It is more common in boys than girls, ie, between the ages of five to ten years it is 6.9 per cent for boys and 2.8 per cent for girls. Prevalence increases with age. Between the ages of 11 and 16 years conduct disorder was found to occur in 6.6 per cent of the population (8.1 per cent for boys and 5.1 per cent for girls). In addition, problems with behaviour are more frequent in children with learning disabilities.

what is the impact of conduct disorder?

Conduct disorder carries high costs for both the child or young person and their family as well as for society in general. It is associated with poor academic achievement, low self-esteem, low frustration tolerance, poor social skills, depressive symptoms and an increased risk of abuse by parents (A48). These children and young people are more likely to truant from school and more likely to be in trouble with the police. As adults they are more likely to have increased rates of substance abuse, mental health disorders, relationship breakdown and unemployment they also are more likely to commit crime and are more likely to abuse their children. It is rare to find an antisocial adult who did not have conduct problems as a child.

Appropriate parenting styles and early intervention when problems have been identified are highly significant in relation to later outcomes.

• further reading

Scott S, Knapp M, Henderson J and Maughan B (2001) 'Financial Cost of Social Exclusion: Follow-up study of antisocial children into adulthood'. *British Medical Journal* 323.

development and course of conduct disorder

As was noted at the beginning of this text, research suggests that individual, biological, genetic and environmental factors play a part (A16). One of the most important factors that has been identified, reinforced by our new knowledge on the development of the infant brain and for which there is considerable scope in terms of intervention, is the parenting that a child receives. For example, parental coerciveness, harshness and lack of nurturing or appropriate controlling occur more commonly in families with conduct-disordered children and are predictive of disordered behaviour. Conversely, the availability of an emotionally responsive care-giving adult is protective (A42).

• **further reading**

For the classic, original reference for this work, see: Patterson G (1982) *Coercive Family Processes: A social learning approach*. Eugene, Oregon: Castalia.

risk factors for conduct disorder

Risk factors for conduct disorder may be considered in terms of these child, parenting and environmental factors (A42):

child factors
- temperament
- genetic factors
- physical illness
- cognitive deficits
- poor social skills

parenting factors
- poor parenting skills
- poor parental responsiveness
- mental health problems in parents
- substance misuse and criminality in parents
- teenage parenthood
- abuse
- marital discord or violence

environmental factors
- social disadvantage
- homelessness
- low economic status

Some children and young people appear to have a number of factors associated with an increased risk of developing conduct disorder and yet do not go on to develop such behaviours. Factors that have been shown to protect children and young people include:
- an ability to elicit positive responses from people
- an ability to engage with others
- good communication skills
- an ability to respond and relate to substitute caregivers
- a high IQ
- parents with caregiving skills that lead to competence and self-esteem (A42).

Conduct disorder can be divided into early onset (at least one of the defining behaviours present before age of 10) and adolescent onset (none of the defining behaviours present before age of 10) (O1). Less than 50 per cent of children with conduct disorder will go on to be antisocial adults, although the likelihood of disordered conduct continuing into adulthood has been shown to be higher for those with early onset conduct disorder. Moffitt reviews the research that supports this developmental approach in Causes of Conduct Disorder and Juvenile Delinquency (C9).

childhood onset conduct disorder

Children with childhood onset conduct disorder tend to be mostly male (see practice question two, 'What are the gender differences?') and the incidence is not related to socio-economic status. They tend to be more aggressive than young people with adolescent onset conduct disorder.

Findings from literature and clinical consultations in Ontario showed that although only three to five per cent of young people with conduct disorder had showed symptoms in childhood; those who had were thought to account for at least half of the offences committed by young offenders (A10).

adolescent onset conduct disorder

In adolescent onset conduct disorder, it appears that the socio-cultural factors, such as the influence of poverty and peer groups, play a significant role in the escalation of their conduct disordered behaviours. Oppositional and illegal behaviours begin during adolescence and tend to take place in a group environment. These adolescents do not usually have severe learning problems, developmental disabilities, neuropsychiatric problems or a family history of antisocial behaviour. The problem behaviours involve less aggression and tend to stop as the young people mature into adulthood. Girls are more likely to present with adolescent onset conduct disorder rather than childhood onset. Anxiety is particularly common in girls who present at this stage (A10).

Jill's story

Jill has always appeared to be a well-adjusted child but in late adolescence her moods changed. She became irritable and argumentative with her family. Jill started spending a lot of time alone and sometimes disappeared for long periods without saying where she was going. She was verbally abusive to her mother and refused to go to school. Jill self-harmed and was admitted to a psychiatric ward via Accident and Emergency.

When we explore Jill's history we see that Jill has had a reasonably secure childhood though her parents are divorced. However, there have been periods during which she has felt very unsure as to where her home was and which parent and stepparent were taking responsibility for her. In late adolescence Jill's college friend dies suddenly, Jill's grandparents die within a year of one another. Jill's stepmother dies tragically after a short illness. At this point Jill's symptoms become acute.

Jill has some of the features of late onset conduct disorder but is more likely to be diagnosed as being depressed, as her disordered behaviours are not of an overt destructive nature. If these signs are missed Jill may develop further disordered behaviours, which could put her at risk in other ways.

offending behaviour/delinquency

A prospective longitudinal study has examined the development of delinquency and antisocial behaviour in 411 south London boys (B15). The majority were born in 1953 and the study began in 1961. At eight to ten years of age those who we now know went on to become delinquents already differed significantly from non-delinquents. They were more likely to be rated troublesome at primary school, to be from poorer families, supported by social agencies and physically neglected by their parents. They were more likely to have low intelligence, poor school attainment and to be rated as 'daring' by parents and peers.

The most important predictors, at age eight to ten years, of delinquency in adolescence were:

- poor parental child rearing, poor supervision, parental conflict and separation from parents
- hyperactivity
- low intelligence/poor school attainment
- family history of criminality including siblings with behaviour problems
- low family income, large family size and poor housing.

The best independent predictors of chronic offending at age eight to ten years up to age 32 were 'troublesomeness', 'daring' or having a delinquent sibling or a convicted parent (B15).

For boys from vulnerable backgrounds the most protective factors against offending were the avoidance of contact with other troublesome boys in the neighbourhood, and an absence of convicted fathers and delinquent siblings. However, the non-convicted vulnerable males at the age of 32 were not necessarily leading successful lives. Social isolation at age eight seemed to lead on to social isolation at age 32 (B15).

summary of the evidence of the effectiveness of psychosocial interventions for the management of conduct disorder

Research and practice consensus indicates that successful management of children and young people with conduct disorder must address multiple domains in a co-ordinated manner over a period of time. Some milder forms of challenging behaviour require minor intervention, such as parent training, and social skills problem training (eg, problem-solving) for the child and consultation with schools. Chronic conduct disorder, which is usually childhood onset, requires early intervention, intensive treatment in multiple domains and long-term follow-up (A37).

A range of psychosocial interventions have been shown to be effective in the treatment of conduct disorder. These can be grouped into parent-focused, family/systems-focused, child- or young- person-focused approaches, and school-based approaches.

parent-focused approaches

A wide range of parent training programmes is currently available in the UK. However, their content and approach varies widely as does the expertise of the staff who run them. It is important not to confuse the research evidence demonstrating the effectiveness of structured programmes, delivered by experienced staff, with more informal parenting education classes, which are unlikely to have the same impact. Aspects of parent training programmes that have been shown to be effective with conduct disorder include (B34):

content

- structured sequence of topics, introduced in set order over 8-12 weeks
- subjects such as infant nutrition, play, praise, incentives, setting limits, health and safety, and discipline
- emphasis on promoting sociable, self-reliant child behaviour and calm parenting
- constant reference to parent's own experience and, where relevant, predicaments
- theoretical basis informed by extensive empirical research and made explicit
- detailed manual available to enable replicability.

delivery

- collaborative approach acknowledging parents' feelings and beliefs
- difficulties normalised, humour and fun encouraged

- parents supported to practise new approaches during sessions and through homework
- parent and child seen together in individual family work (just parents in some groups' programmes)
- crèche, good quality refreshments and transport provided if necessary
- practitioners supervised regularly to ensure adherence to the programme and to develop skills.

The findings of a recent systematic review (A4) provide some support for the use of group-based parenting programmes (behavioural, cognitive-behavioural or video tape modelling) to improve the emotional and behavioural adjustment of children under the age of three years. There is limited and equivocal evidence concerning whether the results are maintained over time.

For young children (three to ten years old) with conduct disorder, the programme approach most supported by research evidence is group-based parenting programmes. These parent training programmes have been used successfully in a UK setting. Systematic reviews have concluded that behavioural programmes and community-based group programmes are most effective (A3). A recent systematic review (A3) of parent training programmes for improving behaviour in children between three to ten years found that all the parent training programmes reviewed were effective in producing positive improvements in parental perceptions of their child's behaviour. There is a lack of long-term data, although there is some evidence of positive effects up to three years after intervention.

The 2006 NICE health technology assessment (A35) supports these findings for children with a developmental age of 12 and under.

Parent training with older children (ten years and older) has shown smaller effects than for younger children. For this older group, family approaches (using multimodal and cognitive methods to change family behavioural and cognitive patterns) have been more successful (A18).

There is some evidence that addressing parental problems alongside parenting programmes may increase the effectiveness of these programmes although more research is needed in this area.

Drop-out rates of parents from parenting programmes can be high (approximately 40 per cent) and many parents are not able to benefit from such programmes. Accessibility and acceptability of the service need to be considered. Since co-morbidity, (ie, more than one medical or psychiatric condition being present) is common in children with conduct problems and their families, a single approach (such as parent training) is unlikely to solve all problems (C15).

The NICE health technology assessment (A35), looking at the effectiveness and cost-effectiveness of parent training/education programmes for the treatment of conduct disorders (including oppositional defiant disorder) in children with a developmental age of 12 and under, found that, on the balance of evidence, parent training/education programmes appear to be an effective and potentially cost-effective therapy. However, the relative effectiveness and cost-effectiveness of different models of parent training/ education programmes (such as intensity of therapy and setting) require further investigation.

The majority of studies examined in the NICE assessment were in North America or Australia, and the results may not, therefore, be generalisable to the UK. A number of studies that undertook longer-term follow-up, albeit uncontrolled, suggest that the benefit in child behaviour following parent training/education programmes appears to be maintained over time (A35).

family/systems-focused approaches

family therapy

Two reviews have examined the effectiveness of family therapy for children and young people with conduct disorder. The first, a descriptive review (A9), found that family therapy reduced conduct problems and delinquent behaviour in adolescents, when compared to individual therapy or no intervention. However, these results should be treated with caution because the studies included in the review were not all randomised controlled trials. In addition, the review did not include a thorough search of the literature (A59).

The second review, a systematic review of family therapy for children aged 10-17 with conduct disorder or delinquent behaviour (A59), included studies that had evaluated a range of interventions including parent training, family therapy, multisystemic therapy and multidimensional intervention foster care (MTFC). In seven of the eight studies, the participants were referred by juvenile justice systems in the USA and were considered to be serious offenders; the remaining study included participants who had been assessed as having conduct disorder. The results of the systematic review showed:

- A decrease in the number of re-arrests for the young people who received family or parenting interventions compared to other treatment (in five of the included studies), although the authors warn that these results should be interpreted with caution because of the heterogeneity of the pooled data.
- Family and parenting interventions significantly reduced the amount of time spent in institutions compared to those who received the institutions' usual interventions (four studies).

functional family therapy

Functional Family Therapy (FFT) is a highly structured, outcome-driven prevention/intervention programme for young people aged 11-18 years who have challenging behaviour including delinquency, violence, substance misuse, conduct disorder or oppositional defiant disorder. FFT emphasises approaches that enhance protective factors and reduce risk, including the risk of treatment termination. The programme has clearly identified steps which build on each other in order to produce change (A1). The major goal of FFT is to improve family communication and supportiveness while decreasing the intense negativity so often present in these families.

Research from the USA indicates that FFT may be effective in treating young people with conduct disorder, ODD, offending behaviours, substance misuse, violent behaviour and in reducing recidivism in adolescents with histories of multiple offences, as well as preventing younger children in the family from entering care. Effective delivery of this treatment requires considerable training and supervision (A18). For the majority of referrals FTT requires as few as eight to twelve hours of direct service time and generally no more than 26 hours of direct service time for the most severe problem behaviours. The programme is delivered by teams of one or two staff to clients in home settings, clinics and juvenile courts. More UK-based research would be required before this approach could be widely implemented in the UK (A18).

multidimensional treatment foster care (MTFC)

MTFC is known by a range of names including treatment foster care, wrap-around foster care, therapeutic foster care and specialist foster care. It is used to address the needs of children and young people with a history of chronic antisocial behaviour, delinquency or emotional disturbance. It has been shown to reduce the rate of recidivism, to increase placement stability and to improve social skills (A58). Coram Family's Fostering New Links Project (B4), undertaken in London, is similar and shows considerable benefits for the young people involved. However, it makes a heavy demand on staff and foster carers.

ongoing MTFC research

The DfES has funded a MTFC project (running from 2002-2006) with looked after children aged 12 to 16 years. It aims to provide a wrap-around, multilevel programme for young people with complex needs and includes:

- *specially trained and supported foster carers*
- *an individual therapist for each young person*
- *a family therapist to work with the birth and adoptive family*
- *skills trainers to coach and promote social skills*
- *education staff to work at school.*

*The evaluation team, co-directed by Nina Biehal and Jonathan Green at
the Social Work Research and Development Unit (SWRDU) York
University, is comparing outcomes for 12-16 year-olds in MTFC
placements with those for similar young people in a range of alternative
placements (the 'service as usual'). The study is taking place in 15
English local authorities and the evaluation will conclude in 2007. The
project aims to improve the life chances for these young people,
promote greater placement stability and reduce the number of looked
after children in and out of county/borough placements or in specialist
residential, custodial or psychiatric settings.*
*The same team is evaluating the Youth Justice Board's Intensive
Fostering pilot project, which also uses the MTFC model, in three
English authorities. Outcomes for young people placed in Intensive
Fostering will be compared to those for similar persistent young
offenders placed in other settings. This study is due to end in February
2008.*

multisystemic therapy

Multisystemic Therapy (MST) is an intensive family and community-
based treatment that addresses the multiple determinants of serious
behaviour problems. The multisystemic approach views individuals as
nested within a complex network of interconnected systems that
encompass individual, family and community (peer, school and
neighbourhood) factors. Interventions may be necessary in any or a
combination of these systems. MST aims to promote behaviour
change in the young person's natural environment, using the
strengths of each system to facilitate change. MST is provided using a
home-based model of service delivery. The usual duration of MST is
approximately 60 hours of contact over four months. Evaluations of
MST for serious young offenders have shown:
- reductions of 25-70 per cent in long-term re-arrest rates
- reductions of 47-64 per cent in out-of-home placements
- extensive improvements in family functioning
- decreased mental health problems (A22).

MST has been found to be the most effective treatment for
delinquent adolescents in reducing recidivism and improving
individual and family pathology. However the majority of research to
date is based on a highly manualised and intensive programme in the
USA. MST has recently been used in Belfast and Cambridge in the UK.
A description of the Cambridge project, including an evaluation, can
be accessed on the YoungMinds website at: www.youngminds.
org.uk/magazine/71/squire.php

A Cochrane review (A30) of the results of eight randomised
controlled trials of MST (conducted in the USA, Canada and Norway),

however, indicates that it is premature to draw conclusions about the effectiveness of MST compared with other services. The review found that results were inconsistent across studies that varied in quality and context and concluded that there is no information about the effects of MST compared with no treatment. It also found no harmful effects from MST.

This apparent contradiction reflects the fact that robust studies are few and in many ways not comparable. Some of the studies in the Cochrane review showed positive effects but these were not seen across them all.

child-or young-person-focused approaches

There are a number of different types of child- or young-person-focused interventions, both group-based and one-to-one. However, there is evidence that group-based treatments for conduct disorders in adolescents may lead to an increase in behavioural problems (A12, A18).

The remainder of this section is therefore focused on individual approaches, which are likely to be more effective.

cognitive behavioural and behavioural therapies

Cognitive behavioural programmes cover a broad range of therapies. They are usually highly structured and relatively brief (6-24 sessions). Cognitive therapy employs techniques for addressing problematic thoughts, assumptions and beliefs, while behavioural therapies use psychological principles to achieve behavioural goals. Cognitive behavioural therapy (CBT) combines these approaches.

Cognitive behavioural therapy approaches include:
- behaviour modification (reinforcing behaviours through reward)
- moral reasoning enhancement (through group discussion)
- social skills training, such as problem-solving skills (including modelling, role-play, coaching and feedback)
- self-instruction (improving self-control and reducing impulsiveness).

None of the single-component or single-focus individual skills programmes has been demonstrated to be effective in the treatment of young people with conduct disorders and using more than one approach simultaneously may prove more effective. Mild conduct problems may be ameliorated with the help of social skills and anger management coping skills training, but there is no evidence for the use of these approaches on their own or with more chronic and severe cases (A18).

Problem-solving skills training is one of the best evaluated cognitive-behavioural approaches for the treatment of conduct problems. Its effectiveness in combination with parent training has been demonstrated by two studies and this would seem to be the treatment of choice for severe conduct problems in children aged eight to twelve years (A18). There is, however, often a problem with large drop-out rates from combined approaches of this nature. A Barriers to Treatment Measure has been designed (C1) and this offers the potential for devising specific interventions aimed at the therapeutic engagement of families at high risk of drop-out (A18).

Among adolescents, schemes encompassing cognitive behavioural therapy techniques have been found to be effective in both juvenile justice and non-juvenile justice settings (A18). Cognitive behavioural therapy has been shown to be particularly successful for adolescents who are offending. The literature shows that behavioural intervention on its own yields a significantly greater effect than non-behavioural treatment. For example it may reduce re-offending by 10 per cent to 20 per cent (A28).

The effects of treatment are greater for young people who had a mixed background of offending (as opposed to mainly property offences) and for serious offenders. As with other interventions, short, intensive programmes have been found to have poorer results than longer programmes with regular but less intensive contact (A28).

A review of media-based therapies (A33), based on the premise that access to treatments is limited due to factors such as time and expense, concluded that media-based cognitive-behavioural therapies for any young person with a behavioural disorder are worth considering in clinical practice. Presenting the information parents need in order to manage these behaviour problems in booklet or other media-based format would most likely reduce the cost and increase access.

traditional psychotherapy

A systematic review of psychoanalytic approaches to treatment concluded that young people with disruptive behaviours and externalising problems were more difficult to treat than children and young people with emotional disorders. Younger children (under the age of 12) were more likely to benefit from intensive treatment approaches but no clear benefits were associated with intense treatment approaches for adolescents (A27).

mentoring

Mentoring has been proposed as a method for dealing with juvenile delinquency, antisocial behaviour and school drop-out. There is little evidence that it has a positive effect in this area (A45). A review undertaken for the Youth Justice Board (B33) shows that, while young people in the justice system found the relationship with mentors positive, there was little hard evidence to suggest that it had a significant effect on levels of offending.

school-based approaches

In the UK, the special educational needs (SEN) system may provide a route for identification and treatment of children with conduct disorder. Current policy states that children who have emotional or behavioural difficulties should be retained within mainstream schools with behaviour management plans in place wherever possible, although the value of this has recently been challenged by its architect, Baroness Mary Warnock. Lady Warnock published a fundamental rethink of the process in 2005, which highlights that pressure to include pupils with problems in mainstream schools causes 'confusion of which children are the casualties' - with teachers' resources overstretched to the detriment of all pupils in the class (O6).

A range of intervention programmes has been developed to address challenging behaviour in schools, but many have not been based on research evidence and some are not consistent with intervention strategies used in the home setting (A18). Some school-based interventions focus on particular problem behaviours, such as bullying, while others address a range of conduct problems (A48). Success has been reported in anti-bullying programmes although this has been found to vary greatly between schools (A18). Some school-wide programmes to prevent bullying do show promise (in quasi-experimental studies) for reducing the levels of aggression within schools, but their effect on the prevalence of aggressive behaviour of clinical severity is unknown (A18). Peer support programmes may also offer successful ways to combat bullying behaviours (B12).

In general, strong positive leadership, high pupil expectations, close monitoring of pupils, good opportunities to engage in school life and take on responsibility, well-functioning incentive reward and punishment systems, high levels of parental involvement, an academic emphasis and a focus on learning are factors that are associated with schools with lower levels of behaviour problems (A18).

Where children have behavioural problems in the classroom, the addition of contingency management programmes (covering contingency management techniques, such as the use of behavioural contracts, reinforcement for work completed, and physical reorganisation of classrooms) may be considered, in addition to family-based treatment (A18). Interventions that improve the classroom management skills of teachers (contingency management techniques, such as the use of behavioural contracts, reinforcement for work completed and physical reorganisation of classrooms) have been shown to have the potential to impact on child behaviours. A recognised problem of relying solely on school-delivered interventions is that behavioural changes have been found not to generalise to other settings (A18).

Reviews of the impact of in-school interventions for young people with a range of problem behaviours have found that out-of-class CBT and social competence training – with or without cognitive behavioural components – produced significant, positive change (A18).

A meta-analysis conducted in the USA (A57) cautions that the majority of research addressing school-based intervention programmes to reduce aggressive and disruptive behaviour in schools deals almost exclusively with demonstration programmes. The effects found in practice programmes were small, considerably smaller than those found in demonstration projects. Interventions were generally more effective when they were implemented well, relatively intense, one-to-one and administered by teachers (A57). Adequate training of staff and supervision and support were also considered to be crucial for successful implementation.

A review of interventions to support pupils with emotional and behavioural difficulties in mainstream primary schools (A15) also concluded that the evidence base for recommending effective strategies that teachers could draw on was limited, but identified the following approaches which had been shown to be effective by at least one robust study:

- Behavioural strategies using token systems for delivering rewards and sanctions, either to the whole class or to individuals, for reducing disruptive behaviour (boys and girls aged seven to ten years in the USA).
- A relatively short cognitive behavioural programme, delivered outside the classroom, to train children in self-instruction, can reduce disruptive behaviour; and these reductions can be sustained over time (boys and girls aged seven to ten years in the USA).
- Multisession interventions delivered by specialist personnel to help children cope with anger, produced short-term reduction in aggressive behaviour (boys and girls aged nine to twelve in the USA).
- A multisession social skills programme delivered by regular classroom teachers can produce short-term positive effects on social skills, but results were not maintained in the long term (boys and girls aged nine to twelve years in Australia).

Intervening Early (B3) is a short report specifically for primary schools. While not addressing the current needs of the older age group, it provides a useful digest of current practice. It looks at ways of supporting children who are finding it difficult to get the best out of their time at school, helps schools to assess their present situation, identifies the issues that may be contributing to the difficulties children face and explores different approaches to helping them overcome those difficulties. The report describes four types of intervention in detail, and gives some indication of where each is most appropriately used. The four types are:

- a whole school approach
- small groups
- one-to-one
- work with parents.

The report also examines how schools have intervened successfully to help children with difficulties, what is available to enable a school to intervene, what will be suitable in different kinds of situation for different children, and what kinds of effect may be expected from an intervention. Information was received from 120 education authorities and schemes in England and from 55 Education Action Zones. Thirty-five field visits were made to schools using some of the more commonly used interventions. The report does not rank the effectiveness of the various interventions, some of which have been comprehensively evaluated, nor does it cover every possible intervention. However it describes systematic approaches to identifying children who have difficulties and to providing them with extra support.

Evidence to suggest that social work might make a valuable contribution to keeping children in school (B36) is limited, but the development of the multiprofessional Behaviour and Education Support Teams (BESTs) looks promising (see practice question 9, 'How can we help children and young people to stay in school?'). BESTs bring together staff across a number of agencies. Although the make up of each team will vary from locality to locality, it will almost always include educational psychologists, social workers, education welfare officers and child and adolescent mental health workers who aim to support pupils who are experiencing, or are vulnerable to, emotional and behavioural difficulties and the problems that may arise from these.

A 2005 evaluation of BESTs identifies many benefits of multiagency working but also cautions that BEST staff need training to operate effectively in a multiagency way and that location, accommodation and communication links between schools and the team are key issues if the work is to be effective. To see the evaluation, go to: www.dfes.gov.uk/best/uploads/RR706.pdf

• further reading

Evans J, Harden A, Thomas J and Benefield P (2003) *Support for pupils with Emotional and Behavioural Difficulties (EBF) in Mainstream Primary School Classrooms: A systematic review of the effectiveness of interventions.* London: EPPI Centre and NFER

a brief note on diet

There has been a renewed interest in diet as a factor in mental health with the publication of reports (see 'Further Reading' below) drawing together the evidence for this. The importance of fatty acids – omega 3 and omega 6 – is highlighted, as is the increasing presence in today's diet of trans-fats, such as commercially made cakes and crisps, which adversely affect the brain's ability to use these vital nutrients.

A study of particular relevance here (B18) noted that improvements in the diets of 231 young offenders were linked to a drop of 26 per cent in antisocial behaviour incidents and a 37 per cent reduction in violent offences.

further reading

Cornah, D (2006) *Feeding Minds: The impact of food on mental health.* London: The Mental Health Foundation

Raine A, Mellingen K, Jianghong L, Venables P and Mednick S (2003) 'Effects of environmental enrichment at ages 3-5 on schizotypal personality and antisocial beahviour at ages 17 and 23 years' *American Journal of Psychiatry 160*

Van de Weyer, C (2005) *Changing Diets, Changing Minds: How food affects mental well-being and behaviour.* London: Sustain

conclusions

The evidence on conduct disorder is difficult to summarise because of the range of different definitions of the problem, often linked to the backgrounds of the researchers. This situation, and indeed the constant debate over the nature of conduct disorder, is not helpful for practitioners who are trying to work with these children and young people or, more importantly, for the children and young people themselves. Lack of agreement and clarity of terms also serves as a barrier to undertaking successful systematic reviews, which are valuable tools to assist decision making, and aim to pull together research findings into clear messages for practitioners.

It is clear that the best time to tackle conduct disorder is when the child is very young. Improving parent-child attachments, promoting sensitive and responsive parenting, and providing structured parent training programmes are the most effective interventions.

Although the evidence shows that established patterns of behaviour are more resistant to change, this review identifies interventions that may help older children and young people with established conduct disorder.

It is concerning that the messages that can be applied from research in this field are frequently hampered by the poor quality, or non-existence, of primary research studies. Improved collaboration between researchers and practitioners and between research commissioners and practitioners would go some way to rectifying this situation for the future. Lack of evidence of effectiveness does not necessarily imply that an intervention is ineffective.

However some clear messages have emerged regarding the provision of interventions for older children and young people with conduct disorder. Services need to be able to offer, or have access to, a range of psychosocial interventions, depending on the age, developmental stage and individual circumstances of each child or young person. As the behavioural problems become more severe, the availability of multimodal approaches, which engage with the child or young person, their family and their wider environment/systems (such as their school) become increasingly important.

While these are important messages to inform service planning and delivery, a factor that is not highlighted in randomised controlled trials but is of interest is the recognition of the importance of the potential for any individual adult to influence the life of any young person. This, however, is a factor that is frequently described by adults who, as children, were exposed to many of the risk factors for conduct disorder or antisocial behaviour, but who proved to be resilient (A2).

• further reading

Davis C, Marin G, Kosky R and O'Hanlon A (2000) *Early Intervention in the Mental Health of Young People: A literature review*. Adelaide: The Australian Early Intervention Network for Mental Health in Young People. Online version available at: http://auseinet.flinders.edu.au

Evans J, Harden A, Thomas J and Benefield P (2003) *Support for Pupils with Emotional and Behavioural Difficulties (EBD) in Mainstream Primary School Classrooms: A systematic review of the effectiveness of interventions*. London: EPPI Centre and NFER

Fonagy P, Target M, Cottrell D, Phillips J and Kurtz Z (2002) *What Works for Whom: A critical review of treatments for children and adolescents*. New York: The Guildford Press

Kowalenko N, Barnett B, Fowler C and Matthey S (2000). 'The Perinatal Period: Early interventions for mental health' in *Clinical Approaches and Early Intervention in Child and Adolescent Mental Health, Volume 4*. Adelaide: Australian Early Intervention Network for Mental Health in Young People. Online version available at: http://auseinet.flinders.edu.au

Richardson J and Joughin C (2002) *Parent Training Programmes for the Management of Young Children with Conduct Disorder: Findings from research*. London: Gaskell.

research messages for ten common practice questions

This review has been produced as a direct response to questions submitted by practitioners in the **research** in **practice** network of Partner agencies. Examples of research and local programmes are provided to illustrate areas of practice relevant to each question.

question 1

should the approach to conduct disorder be different for children and young people of different ages?

The choice of management approach will depend on the child's age, type and severity of problem, their strengths and cognitive ability and their ability to engage in therapy (A10).

As a general rule parent training is the treatment of choice for behavioural problems in children under eight years of age, particularly for those cases of mild and moderate severity, less co-morbidity (more than one medical or psychiatric condition being present) and less social disadvantage. Group-based parent training programmes have been shown to be more successful in improving the behaviour of children aged three to ten years, compared with methods that involved working with parents on an individual basis (A4, A35).

For older children (up to approximately 12 years of age) and for more severe presentations, research suggests that parent training should be combined with individual cognitive behavioural therapy interventions that provide problem solving and social skills training (A58).

Parent training for behavioural problems in adolescents (including 14 and 15 year olds) appears to have limited effectiveness in moderating behaviour when used in isolation. Individual approaches for adolescents, if used either on their own or in combination with systemic interventions, should focus on reducing opportunities for delinquent behaviour and on increasing skills such as problem solving (A58).

For young people at the more extreme end of the challenging behaviour spectrum who are offending, re-offending rates are most likely to be reduced by multimodal behavioural and skills orientated programmes. The strongest evidence is for the use of multilevel relatively intensive community-based, highly structured and well-integrated programmes focusing on changes that reduce opportunities for offending (eg, family monitoring and supervision of the young person). A recent systematic review (A59) found that family and parenting interventions significantly reduced the time spent by juvenile delinquents in institutions. There was a significant decrease in the risk of being re-arrested and a decrease of risk of incarceration.

The types of interventions that appeared to be most successful were multisystemic therapy (MST) and multidimensional foster care (see p20-22 for a full description).

Group treatments for adolescents with behavioural problems are not recommended (A18).

conclusions

Using chronological age alone as a guide to management decisions is not necessarily helpful, as the way in which children respond to interventions will depend on their developmental age and home situation. The approach needs to be tailored to the individual child or young person. However, it would appear that interventions that incorporate parent training and individual cognitive behavioural therapy may be effective for children up to the age of 12, and young people over that age may respond to individual cognitive behavioural interventions. If the conduct disorder is severe it is likely that interventions will only succeed if they are comprehensive and address the many causes of the behavioural problems.

Major barriers for the successful implementation of such programmes are the current lack of practitioners who are trained in cognitive behavioural therapy and the fact that very few services are available that are resourced and staffed to address the complex needs of children and young people with severe behavioural problems. This creates real difficulties for practitioners who have identified the need for intervention but are unable to access the appropriate support for the young person. They may find themselves 'holding' the young person in the interim, an activity which – in itself – may be positive if undertaken with real commitment.

question 2
what are the gender differences?

There is relatively little research on gender differences to guide practice on interventions for girls with conduct disorder. Historically, boys have been more likely to develop conduct disorder with a ratio of three to four boys for every girl with clinically significant problems. Gender differences in aggression have been reported in children diagnosed as young as two to three years of age (A48); boys becoming increasingly more aggressive than girls throughout the primary school period. Gender differences persist during early and middle school years but start to diminish in adolescence. Girls, however, develop late-onset, non-aggressive conduct problems at a greater rate than do boys (A48).

A distinction has been made between antisocial behaviour with biological, as opposed to social, roots (C10). Antisocial behaviour driven by neurodevelopmental causes is more common in boys. This form, with strong genetic and biological influences, is less prevalent, but shows early onset and ongoing persistence. It also seems to have strong genetic and biological influences. Another type of antisocial behaviour, which fluctuates more by circumstances, affects girls as well as boys, and emerges in later years in the context of social relationships.

Gender-related differences in the prevalence of behaviour problems also may partly reflect a biologically based predisposition for boys to react to stressful situations with conduct disordered behaviour such as aggression. Differences are also likely to be related to gender-biased parenting practices that are common in Western cultures. For example, parents may tend to use more physical discipline with boys and more warmth toward girls and to show greater prohibition of aggressive behaviour in their relationship with girls. Girls have been shown to use more verbal negotiation during conflicts than boys and this may prevent the escalation of conflicts into major aggression (A48).

Research undertaken in the USA indicates that female adjudicated delinquents (girls who have been through the criminal justice system) have significantly higher rates of psychopathology, maltreatment history and familial risk factors than males. This research points to the need to address the mental health needs of girls who are young offenders (C8).

One US study (C4) notes that a combination of hyperactivity and unhelpfulness in girls increases their risk of conduct disorder in mid-adolescence whereas, although these traits were also present in boys at risk, the single dimension of hyperactivity predicted conduct disorder in boys.

Attention has generally focused on boys who form the vast majority of those formally excluded from school. Nationally, girls comprise just

17 per cent of permanent exclusions. Many more girls are excluded either informally or for a fixed period. There has been little research focusing on the experiences and specific needs of girls in relation to their disaffection with education. There is growing evidence of unofficial and informal exclusions, and girls appear more vulnerable to these types of exclusions than boys. Unofficial exclusions remain largely hidden and are absent from official statistics. Research (B29) examining girls' perceptions of school life and the use of exclusion in various forms, both official and unofficial, identified that (2001):

- Girls were not generally a priority in schools thinking about behaviour management and school exclusion.
- The invisibility of girls' difficulties had serious consequences for their ability to get help. Resources tended to be targeted at boys. However, the nature of the support on offer to girls and their own responses when in difficulty could also lead to them not receiving help. In addition many girls were unwilling to take up current forms of support and many providers did not refer them because they believed existing provision was inappropriate for girls.
- A number of experiences affected girls disproportionately or exclusively and may adversely have affected their ability to attend and achieve in school, placing them at greater risk of exclusion. These included pregnancy and caring responsibilities.
- Self-exclusion and internal exclusion (for example, truancy or being removed from the classroom) appeared to be widespread.
- Bullying was a serious problem and appears to be a significant factor in girls' decisions to self-exclude. However, bullying among girls was not easily recognised and there was often an institutional failure to tackle bullying among girls effectively.

A literature review noted that conduct disorder is 'a relatively common psychiatric diagnosis and appears to be associated with several serious outcomes, such as antisocial personality disorder and early pregnancy' (A26). The authors suggest that what distinguishes conduct disorder in girls is 'the high risk they have of developing co-morbid conditions, especially internalizing disorders.'

conclusions

Recent headlines have highlighted the increasing incidence of antisocial behaviour and severe forms of aggression among girls. More research is needed to understand and provide effective responses to conduct disorder for these young people. In the meantime the practitioner should bear in mind the apparent gender differences in conduct disorder manifestations, particularly the likelihood in girls of co-morbid and/or internalising disorders, in order to respond appropriately to both girls and boys.

question 3
how should behavioural problems be managed for young people with learning disabilities[1]?

Learning disabilities may be caused by a range of factors, such as brain injury at birth, infections that affect the brain after birth or genetic disorders. About three in a thousand children have moderate or severe learning disabilities. Within this group approximately 50 per cent are thought to suffer from significant mental health problems (A8). Learning disability includes the presence of:

- a significantly reduced ability to understand new or complex information, to learn new skills (impaired intelligence), with
- a reduced ability to cope independently (impaired social functioning), and
- impairment that started before adulthood, with a lasting effect on development (D6).

The mental health needs of young people with learning disabilities have frequently gone unrecognised and they have not received appropriate support. Standard 9 of the *National Service Framework for Children, Young People and Maternity Services* (D7) highlights these young people as a group that requires particular attention as they frequently fall between service provision from child and adolescent mental health services and learning disability psychiatry; consequently they receive insufficient care and support.

A significant number of children and young people with learning disabilities display behaviours such as aggression against others, self-injury, and property destruction. The prevalence of aggressive behaviour has been investigated in only a few published studies. Community surveys of people with learning disability in the UK have shown that physical aggression and destruction of property were identified in 43 per cent of people with learning disabilities who presented with various types of problem behaviours (A21).

Research indicates that severe behavioural problems in people with learning disabilities often have multiple causes and effects (A40). The impact on families of having children with learning disabilities who present severe problem behaviour should not be underestimated. The stress on the family is considerable and can frequently lead to family breakdown and the removal of the child from the family (D11). Research highlights the importance of developing early intervention services for these children and young people as well as the importance of nurturing both the child and the family (A39, C2). Children with learning disabilities and problem behaviours are much more likely to be admitted to residential care (C13).

1 The use of the term learning disability and learning difficulties is largely specific to the UK. Researchers from outside the UK use terms such as 'mental retardation' and 'development disability' to describe largely the same problems. In the past the term 'mentally handicapped' also described the same group of children.

It has long been recognised that even the most destructive behaviours are often learned because they are reinforced in some way. Challenging behaviour may also be considered to be a form of communication (A5). Management of challenging behaviour needs to address:

- the provision of alternative methods for communication
- skills training to support self-management to promote good behaviour
- anger management training
- treatment of depression if required (A5).

Evidence from a range of studies suggests that similar family factors may be implicated in the development of challenging behaviour in children and young people with developmental disability and the development of conduct disorder in children and young people without developmental disability (Tonge 2004). For example increased prevalence of challenging behaviour has been associated with:

- discontinuities in upbringing, family discord and instability or disorganisation in the home among young adults with mild developmental disabilities
- poor parental adjustment and parent-child relationships among children with developmental disabilities
- inadequate housing, low income and unemployment among families with a child with Down Syndrome.

These studies examine challenging behaviour in children and young people with mild developmental disabilities. It is not known whether severe disabilities, especially when accompanied by physical impairments, amplify or overshadow the impact of such factors (A52).

A co-operative working relationship with the parents will make it more likely that they will feel encouraged to share their grief regarding their child's disability. This in itself can be therapeutic. In addition, counselling and the provision of psychological and educational interventions for siblings may also be necessary to promote family functioning (A52).

It should be remembered that children with learning disability can suffer from the full range of mental health problems experienced by other children and young people of normal intelligence. As the level of disability becomes more severe, however, it becomes increasingly difficult for the clinician to apply existing diagnostic classifications with confidence.

While there is now a considerable body of evidence to guide practitioners on the management of a range of child and adolescent mental health problems, there is not a comparable body of evidence on the effectiveness of interventions for children and adolescents with learning and developmental disabilities. Indeed the existing evidence on the efficacy of cognitive behavioural and behavioural interventions on aggression in children and adults with learning disabilities has been described as scant, with a paucity of methodologically sound clinical trials. One systematic review (A21) conducted in 2003 was only able to identify three studies (adult based) which met the inclusion criteria. The findings indicated that direct interventions based on cognitive behavioural methods (modified relaxation, assertiveness training with problem solving, and anger management) appeared to have some impact on reduction of aggressive behaviour at the end of treatment but not at six-month follow-up as rated by individuals and their carers (A21).

Established patterns of aggressive behaviour usually require intensive and individualised management. Interventions include:
• enrichment of environment
• rescheduling activities
• differential reinforcement of other behaviours
• anger management
• problem solving
• individual or group cognitive behavioural therapy (A21).

Successful management begins with the establishment of a positive relationship with the parents and carers and if possible the children and young people. A working diagnosis that takes into account the biological, psychological and social contributing factors and context provides the key to a rational management plan. Treatment is usually multimodal, requiring a combination of parent support and skills training, behavioural interventions, modification to the social and educational environment, and modified psychological treatments (A52).

There is no evidence that family therapy has a direct effect, but it may reduce family dysfunction and conflict and modify problematic family interactional patterns, such as parental overprotection, which contribute to psychopathology in the child (A52).

There is some evidence for the effectiveness of behavioural approaches for children and young people with learning disabilities and behavioural problems. The design of an effective behaviour modification programme requires a detailed behavioural analysis regarding the context, consequences that reinforce the behaviour, the response by others to the behaviour, and the longer term consequences of the behaviour (A52).

Some young people with moderate or less severe levels of developmental disability have sufficient skill and understanding of consequences to be able to benefit from a modified form of cognitive behavioural treatment. This involves a combination of relaxation training, modelling and reinforcement of confident and prosocial behaviour, formulating positive self thoughts and statements instead of negative attributions, and providing a structured experience of rewarding educational and social activities and skills (A52).

conclusions

Children and young people with learning disabilities need access to the same range of mental health services as other children and young people. Needs should be assessed by appropriately trained staff who are able to identify and support both the child or young person and their family when behavioural problems are evident.

The national Child and Adolescent Mental Health Service (CAMHS) mapping exercise (D1) identified that only 45 per cent of services were accessible to children and young people with learning disabilities and three Strategic Health Authority areas were without any specialist learning disability CAMHS provision. This and the fact that the number of young people with learning disabilities seen by CAMHS was just under 8,800 (8 per cent of the total caseload), suggests that there is some way to go to meet the vision of services accessible to young people with mental health difficulties and learning disabilities. This is a key area of concern for CAMH services on the ground and at a policy level.

In order to support the practitioner in this under-resourced environment, the Care Services Improvement Partnership (CSIP: www.icesdoh.org/default.asp) has established a Do Once and Share project, lead by Professor Panos Vostanis, to develop a care pathway that will support professionals, and give parents and carers more confidence and a vision early on of what support and care they can expect. The final report was completed in May 2006; go to: www.camhs.org.uk/documentdownload.aspx?doc=DOAS%2OLD%2 oCAMHS%2oFinal%2oReport%2ofinal.doc

service examples

Leicestershire & Rutland Beacon Home Intervention Project

This is a home-based highly responsive service providing trained staff to work with parents and carers of children with learning disabilities and challenging behaviour within the home, to model strategies and then to support the families to work with the intervention.

For those families that continued with the project two thirds of problem behaviours were reduced in frequency by 76-100 per cent. A quarter of the behaviours showed improvement of 51-73 per cent and the remainder showed improvement above 25 per cent.

This Home Intervention Project is included as a case study (support for parents) on: www.teachernet.gov.uk/casestudies/casestudy.cfm ?id=23

Challenging Behaviour Team - East Kent Hospital Trust
This is a service for children with learning disabilities who have
challenging behaviour. The Challenging Behaviour Team is headed by
a consultant clinical psychologist and works with child development
centres, child and adolescent mental health services, health visitors,
schools, nursing, education and social services.

It covers children aged between 0 and 19, and referrals are made
via consultant paediatricians, special educational needs officers, child
development teams or special schools. It provides direct help to
families and trains and supports professional staff in different
disciplines. Parents are engaged as active partners in helping the
child and are given copies of all the paperwork about the treatment
plan and its progress.
www.childrensnsfcasestudies.dh.gov.uk/children/nsfcasestudies.nsf

question 4
what is the connection between conduct disorder and substance misuse?

Many children and young people use and experiment frequently with a range of drugs, including alcohol, from early adolescence. While moderate, recreational use may remain unproblematic, sustained, heavy use merits concern. There are temporary risks, however, such as increased risk-taking behaviour, associated with any use. This needs to be borne in mind by the practitioner alongside other concerning factors.

Numerous questionnaires and diagnostic studies have demonstrated associations between adolescent drug and alcohol use and various forms of psychopathology, including low self-esteem, depression, antisocial behaviour, rebelliousness, aggressiveness, crime, delinquency, truancy and poor school performance, conduct disorder, anxiety disorders, depressive disorders, suicide and ADHD. The use of illicit drugs has been shown to be associated with conduct disorder and antisocial behaviour (A13) and the addition of substance misuse to conduct disorder is predictive of violent behaviour for boys. Early treatment for substance misuse is clearly important (A10).

The Strengthening Families Program (SFP): For Parents and Youth aged 10-14 years (www.strengtheningfamilies.org) is a programme used in the USA that aims to reduce substance abuse and behaviour problems during adolescence by improving parental nurturing and limit-setting skills, improving parent-child communication and improving children's pro-social skills. The programme consists of seven sessions and four booster sessions, six months to one year after the original sessions, and was tested in 33 schools. The schools were randomly assigned to one of three conditions: the strengthening families programme, the drug free years programme and a minimal contact control group. Evaluation of this programme has identified:

- Significant parenting outcome differences between intervention and control groups at both 18 months and 30 months
- Significant differences between intervention and control group in substance use, conduct problems, school-related problem behaviours, peer resistance and affiliation, and antisocial peers at 18- and 30-month follow-up
- Significantly delayed initiation of alcohol, tobacco and marijuana use, lower frequency of alcohol and tobacco use and lower levels of overt and covert aggressive behaviours and hostility in interaction with parents in SFP 10-14 children at four-year follow-up (C11).

In drug prevention research there is little knowledge as to what constitutes an effective or ineffective intervention. The available evidence suggests that both broadly based and more specifically focused interventions can have an effect. The provision of booster sessions and multicomponent programmes may have the potential to have a positive effect on drug prevention programmes (A7).

A review undertaken by the Health Development Agency (A54) concluded that school-based alcohol-misuse programmes are ineffective and that there is weak evidence from non-systematic reviews for the effectiveness of parent-based interventions. A later review (A20) found that evidence remains inconclusive, hampered by the poor methodology of the original studies. Most of the research in this area has been conducted in the US, where drug, alcohol and tobacco misuse programmes are often combined with an emphasis on abstinence from all. This is philosophically different from the approach adopted in the UK and most of Europe, and conclusions from this research need to be interpreted with caution. Current research is not consistent regarding the effectiveness of peer-led programmes in this field.

conclusions

The results of the SFP 10-14 programme are promising and further research is needed to see the extent to which it is transferable to the UK. This is an area where prevention is particularly important and a range of drug prevention programmes are now being used in primary schools and secondary schools throughout the UK. It is, however, beyond the scope of this review to detail the various programmes, and the current evidence is unble to identify effective approaches to school-based drug prevention and alcohol prevention education programmes. This is not to say that drugs education programmes in schools are not valid as a component in enabling young people to make positive health choices.

• further reading

Arendt M, Rosenberg R, Foldager L, Perto G and Munk-Jorgensen P (2005) 'Cannabis-induced Psychosis and Subsequent Schizophrenia-spectrum Disorders: Follow-up study of 535 incident cases' *British Journal of Psychiatry* 187

Useful website: Talk to Frank at: www.talktofrank.com is a free, 24-hours-a-day confidential drugs information and advice service.

question 5
what can services do for young people with a history of attachment problems?

Secure attachments underpin the physical and emotional ties that support and sustain us as we grow and develop and can console us in times of distress (A46). There is extensive research linking the type of care that an infant receives during the first few years of life with the development of challenging behaviours (O2). (See also discussion of the research on the developing brain on page 6). Research exploring the links between attachment and disordered behaviour can be divided into two groups: prospective studies that relate infant attachment to later outcomes, and investigations assessing attachment concurrent with disorder (A36).

Children and young people with attachment problems have usually experienced significant disruption in the early years of life and generally feel a profound sense of loss and insecurity. Their behaviour can be extremely challenging and frequently leads to the breakdown of placements (A43).

Attachment theory suggests several specific processes that may be associated with the cause or maintenance of conduct problems. Many of the early disruptive behaviours considered to be precursors of conduct disorder (eg, aggression and non-compliance) may be viewed as attachment orientated behaviours to gain the attention and proximity of caregivers who are otherwise unresponsive. Insecure attachment may also lead to hostility and reactive aggression (A36).

Although there is currently no systematic treatment research that provides a clear basis for specific treatment interventions, behavioural treatment may help older children and young people to enhance their social skills and be more discriminating in their behaviour toward others. It should be noted that children who have experienced problems with attachment do not automatically go on to have disturbed conduct or challenging behaviour (A43).

One programme for adolescents with conduct disorder, called the Response Programme (C7), traces its conceptual roots to attachment theory. This 30-day residential programme is followed by intensive, long-term outreach services in the community that attempt to directly alter the youth's social ecology; for example, a close relationship between the adolescent and an adult role model in a work setting may be cultivated. During the third week of the residential programme discussions focus on attachment issues in the family, including transgenerational attachment patterns. A follow-up study showed significant reductions in adult and youth reported symptoms. However, it should be noted that the study was uncontrolled and that although the programme's goals and procedures were compatible with attachment theory they did not differ substantially from other community outreach programmes emphasising supportive social relationships for troubled youth (A11).

Other programmes, undertaken largely in the USA, have some bearing on conduct disordered behaviour and are useful to consider here. The positive effects of participation in youth organisations are reviewed by Quinn (C12) for example. In an earlier work (1993) the author identifies the presence of a close, confiding relationship as an important protection in adolescence and later life though the evidence suggests that young people, damaged by poor attachment in early years, find these sorts of relationships difficult to enter into. In the absence of more rigorous data the practitioner needs to think carefully about the possibility and importance of constructing such a relationship with the client.

conclusions

The clinical application of attachment theory to conduct disorder is at a very early stage of development. Research is still not clear about at what age it may no longer be possible to reverse the effects of disordered early attachments. Very little is known about attachment-related treatments for older children presenting with early or fully developed forms of conduct disorder and there is currently no evidence for effective interventions for them.

Researchers have described very intensive, psychodynamic psychotherapeutic work with extremely troubled young people whose attachment has been fractured (A18, A19). While the outcomes in small numbers of cases are impressive, the approach is unlikely to be available to many young people. This presents a dilemma for practitioners seeking to provide the best interventions, and underlines the importance of a regular dialogue between social workers and Child and Adolescent Mental Health workers to support decisions about the use of scarce resources.

• further reading

David T, Gouch K, Powell S and Abbott L (2003) *Birth to Three Matters: A review of the literature, compiled to inform the framework to support children in their earliest years.* Research Report 444. London: DfES. Available online at www.dfes.gov.uk/rsgateway/DB/RRP/u013918/index.shtml

Prior V and Glaser D (In Press) *Understanding Attachment and Its Disorders: Theory, evidence and practice.* London: Jessica Kingsley Publishers

Bateman A and Fonagy P (2004) *Psychotherapy for Borderline Personality Disorder: Mentalization based treatment.* Oxford: Oxford University Press

Barth R, Crea T, John K, Thoburn J and Quinton D (2005) 'Beyond Attachment Theory and Therapy: Towards sensitive and evidence-based interventions with foster and adoptive families in distress'. *Child and Family Social Work* 10

question 6
what impact do fathers and stepfathers have on children's behaviour?

Little research is available that specifically addresses the impact of fathers on children's behaviour. However, messages can be drawn from research that explores wider issues relating to the importance of fathers and parenting.

Secondary analysis of data collected in the three British national birth cohort studies concluded that there is reasonable evidence to support the hypothesis that the parent-child relationship is a determinant of both physical and mental health in adult life and that interventions to improve the quality of parent-child relationships could have a pervasive beneficial impact on both physical and mental health. Poor relationships with fathers appeared to have a greater impact on health than poor relationships with mothers (A51).

Researchers have used the National Child Development Study (NCDS) to explore the impact of fathers' involvement with their children when the children were aged 7, 11 and 16. An 'involved father' was defined as one who read to his child, took outings with his child, was interested in his child's education and took an equal role to the mother in managing his child. He may or may not be living with the child's mother and he may or may not be the biological father of the child. Good father-child relations were associated with an absence of emotional and behavioural difficulties in adolescence and greater academic motivation. Boys were less likely to be in trouble with the police if they had an involved father. Involvement of the father also had a significant protective role against psychological problems of adolescents in the families where parents had separated (A17). Descriptive research has also shown that fathers have an important role to play in protecting their children from delinquency (B7).

Research undertaken to explore fathers' involvement, from the perspective of parents and their children in intact and separated families, involved a large-scale survey of children in three secondary schools and their parents, and included in-depth interviews with 26 intact families. This research identified that:

- Children were more likely to experience emotional and behavioural difficulties if there were high levels of conflict between parents.
- Children with non-resident fathers were likely to be less well-adjusted if there were high levels of conflict between parents and if the mother was not very involved with them.
- Fathers perceived sons to be more difficult than daughters. (B38)

A study of 878 33-year-olds bringing up children in stepfamilies (B16) in 1991 found that, contrary to popular perception, stepfathers were often more involved than biological fathers in caring for and bringing up their dependent children. Both biological and stepparents in stepfamilies reported more relationship difficulties and disagreements over child-rearing than their counterparts in first families. In addition the researchers identified that parents in stepfamilies were more vulnerable to depression than those in first families. Overall the findings suggested that today's stepfathers are much more involved in parenting than were their predecessors a generation ago. The findings from this study also point to a need for specific support for parenting in stepfamilies.

Findings from a longitudinal study of a cohort of children born in 1972 and 1973 (B22) indicate that young fathers are more likely to come from families characterised by high conflict, instability and criminality, to have initiated sexual activity at a young age, to have poor reading skills and conduct problems. Regardless of age at first fatherhood, a history of conduct problems and a poor relationship with parents predict that a young man will spend less time with his first-born. This research highlights the importance of identifying and addressing challenging behaviour in order to protect the next generation and break intergenerational cycles of behaviour.

conclusions

Although this is another area that would benefit from further research, the available evidence highlights the importance of fathers in promoting good mental health for their children. Few parenting programmes or other general services are developed to address the needs of fathers. A study undertaken as part of the Sure Start National Evaluation (B25) identified that:

- Fathers are more inclined to attend activities designed specifically for them.
- Services had high levels of father involvement when they had decided early in the planning stage that fathers would be central to their work.
- The presence of a member of staff dedicated to involving fathers led to improved participation.

These messages have the potential to inform other services when planning inclusive services that meet the needs of fathers and value their role in parenting. Attention to the role of fathers is crucial in breaking the cycle of challenging and problematic families (see the story of 'John' on page 11) service example

Children, Fathers and Fatherhood

Children, Fathers and Fatherhood is a three-year Scottish project (2005-2008) that aims to raise awareness of issues affecting children in their relationships with their fathers and to encourage all fathers to develop their fathering skills.

The project is funded by the Scottish Executive and run in partnership with Fathers Direct and the Equal Opportunities Commission.

The project will:

• provide up-to-date information online on policy, projects and services for fathers and professionals
• produce training materials tailored to the needs of fathers and professionals in Scotland
• run conferences, seminars and workshops addressing relevant issues
•inform and influence policy in the best interests of children
www.childreninscotland.org.uk/html/poly_p_fa.htm

question 7
what is the current research on multidisciplinary involvement?

To provide high-quality child-centred care, agencies will need to work in partnership. No one agency has the sole responsibility for supporting children and adolescents with challenging behaviour and conduct disorder. Effective and comprehensive services for these children and adolescents require excellent communication and planning between health, social care, education and youth justice. Commissioning strategies need to provide for care across the age range and will need to be developed collaboratively with a wide range of agencies including Sure Start, voluntary sector agencies, primary health care providers, teachers, child and adolescent mental health specialists, children's services, youth offending teams and Connexions teams, any of which may also be in the local children's trust.

The complexity and variety of service provision for children with challenging behaviour in any one locality may represent a logistical challenge for services attempting to achieve good partnerships. The recent government document *Removing Barriers to Achievement: The Government's Strategy for SEN* (D3) highlights the importance of partnership working to improve outcomes for children and young people with special educational needs (SEN).

Multiagency Behaviour and Education Support Teams (BESTs) have been set up in some areas as part of the DfES's Behaviour Improvement Programme (BIP). The BESTs work with children and young people aged 5-18 to intervene early to address emotional and behavioural problems. These teams can include health workers, social services and the police as well as school representatives. A service example is included in the section on practice question 9, 'How can we help children and young people to stay in school?' For more information on the BIP go to:
www.dfes.gov.uk/ behaviourandattendance

Working together is considered essential to the provision of effective assessment and treatment. For example there is evidence from studies in the treatment of substance misuse that treatment is much less likely to succeed if accompanying psychological problems are not addressed along with the substance misuse (C3, C6).

Over the last 20 years a number of government publications have underlined the importance of joint working in relation to challenging young people. One of the earliest of these is (D8), which still has relevance for today. Progress has been slow but the publication of *Every Child Matters: Change for Children* (D4) and the National Service Framework for Children, Young People and Maternity Services (D7) underlines the government's commitment to ensuring that partnership working is developed.

Recent research undertaken by the Mental Health Foundation to explore partnership working between child and adolescent mental health services (CAMHS) and schools (B28) identified the following factors as facilitating joint working:

- secondments between organisations
- being based in the same location
- flexibility of recruitment so that people move between posts and across organisations
- having a clear understanding of the different roles and expertise of members of staff
- having a clear rationale for joint working, which is shared with the team
- a commitment to joint working from all levels of service
- informal meeting, networking and team building.

Interagency working is a commonly cited mechanism for ensuring child-centred care. A review of the literature on best practice in interagency working (A29), with a focus on collaborative working between local health groups and other agencies, concludes that there is a lack of good evidence on effectiveness of collaborative working, but a good agreement on factors that influence collaboration, either positively or negatively.

This review identifies the following factors as facilitating collaboration:

- commitment of senior personnel
- clearly defined roles and responsibilities
- explicit goals and shared vision
- clarity in lines of accountability
- interagency training, timetable for implementation
- good systems of two-way communication at all levels
- service mapping and evaluation
- shared information
- shared resources, and flexibility.

Factors inhibiting collaboration are: structural, organisational and cultural differences; organisational change; professional differences; personnel change; lack of commitment by agencies or individuals; lack of trust and understanding between agencies and individuals; poor communications within and between agencies and individuals; reluctance or inability to share information; lack of leadership and/or key personnel; limited resources; differences in accountability; loss of power and autonomy; and time pressures.

A systematic review (A32) of effective methods for removing barriers to change to improve collaborative working concluded that there is very little experimental evidence on effectiveness of methods to overcome barriers to change; there is some evidence that shared learning in groups is effective in reducing interprofessional stereotypes between doctors and social workers; there is some weak evidence of effectiveness of quality improvement programmes and interagency training; practical experience of those involved supports the need to prioritise changes, introduce change incrementally and support those involved in change.

A review of evidence of effectiveness of different models of joint working (A6) revealed that the evidence base was limited. Studies did not systematically record process issues or provide evidence of the effects of different models in terms of outcomes. Only four studies met inclusion criteria for the review; none of these focused on children and none provided good evidence of effectiveness of joint working. Evaluations were methodologically poor.

The need for better interagency working is evident in much of the research literature on children in special circumstances. Much research describes inadequacies in current systems of work, though there are also some pointers to effective ways of working. For example, a number of studies have highlighted the beneficial effect of a link worker at the interface between agencies to facilitate communication and improve children's access to services, especially when their needs have traditionally gone unrecognised by services working with adults. An evaluation of a service where primary mental health workers were based in Youth Offending Teams (YOTs), offering a range of direct interventions as well as consultation to YOT staff, found that this model improved young offenders' access to mental health services (B9).

A survey undertaken by the National Institute of Social Work found that collaborative working across organisations has tended to focus on child protection issues, rather than looking at the welfare and needs of the family more broadly. 'Joint' training in this context often means little more than other professionals being able to join child protection staff training sessions, often to learn agency procedures, rather than the notion of continuous professional development (B23).

An evaluation of the Youth Justice Board's Parenting Programme (B19) found that when trying to achieve good interagency working between two previously distinct areas of service provision (such as criminal justice and family support) differences in ethos between sectors and agencies were a real barrier to smooth service development. These differences needed to be acknowledged and worked through at the highest level. Proactive steering groups which met regularly were vital to this process. Large partnerships with many members worked best with strong strategic oversight, and service development was enhanced when the services were not split between sites or managers.

The development of systems to support interagency working to prevent school exclusion has been evaluated in schools with a history of interagency working in three Scottish local authorities (B24). Each of the selected schools identified 30 individual case study pupils for whom interagency initiatives were seen as effective in preventing or reducing exclusion. This research comprised 150 interviews with young people, parents, school staff, other professionals and senior personnel in each authority and highlighted the following points:

- School-based interagency models were central to effective working to reduce exclusion from school.
- Irregular attendance at meetings by key personnel was an issue for all local authorities.
- There was evidence of effective support for young people, which reduced school exclusion, but there was no single answer.
- Being flexible, imaginative and not giving up were crucial to provide support for high maintenance pupils.
- The style of support affected how young people and their families received it. Most viewed support as effective when professionals were informal, equitable and non-judgemental.

conclusions

In general, evidence of outcomes for service users of multiagency working is sparse, although there is some evidence that multidisciplinary teams provide improvements in some outcomes for children and young people and improvements have been shown in staff morale. Research highlights the importance of endeavouring to achieve real interagency working through changes in working practice and changes in culture within organisations rather than 'cherry picking' the elements that are easier to achieve, such as the occasional joint training session.

While boundaries between agencies — particularly in children's services — are changing with the aim of bringing children's services — and in some cases health — in the local authority into one agency, the practitioner will always be required to work across agency boundaries of some sort. The practitioner who can be flexible, who understands the pressures faced by other agencies and can accommodate to these will be more successful in providing a service that is child-centred, as opposed to simply child-focused.

• further reading

Frost N (2005) *Professionalism, Partnership and Joined-up Thinking: A research review of front-line working with children and families.* Dartington: **research** in **practice**

service examples

Essex CAMHS Innovation Project

Working to help looked after children with significant mental health needs who are at risk of experiencing placement breakdown, through the help of a rapid access and multidisciplinary support team providing time-limited interventions extra to local CAMHS.
www.youngminds.org.uk/innovationprojects

Leeds CAMHS Innovation Project

Working to help children and families experiencing child and adolescent emotional problems, and parenting difficulties, through time-limited interventions to families, using a multidisciplinary consultancy team to support Tier 1 staff.
www.youngminds.org.uk/innovationprojects

question 8
how should aggression be managed?

Aggressive behaviour can be defined as behaviour aimed at causing harm to others (A24). Aggressive behaviour in males, and the physical qualities that support it, have long been rewarded (A24). Many of the behaviours that form the criteria for conduct disorder can be viewed as pathological or acceptable depending on the circumstances in which they are performed. Problems occur when children fail to learn, or to apply, rules about the appropriate circumstances in which to use aggression. For example, Pringle's study (B32) of football spectators and mental health shows that watching the game provides a socially acceptable way to release aggression.

Aggressive behaviour may depend on several types of motivation and it is possible that aggression seen in conduct disorder, although involving few inhibitions about hurting others, may spring not just from aggressiveness per se but from other sources – for example the need to seek attention, which could also contribute to other types of antisocial behaviour.

More generalised aggression in childhood, however, can be an early sign of severe disturbance of conduct and is a good predictor of delinquency and behavioural problems in young people. Well over half of future recidivist delinquents can be predicted at the age of seven from their aggressive behaviour, given that their families manifest ineffective childrearing practices. Fighting correlates significantly with lying, and lying predicts stealing behaviour, particularly in adolescents. Assaultive behaviour in childhood has been shown to predict adult imprisonment (A18).

The evidence from a study in the USA showed that early differences in understanding of mind and emotion (assessed when the children were 40 months) were linked to later differences in the children's handling of conflict with their mothers, their siblings and their friends. The children who had been successful in mind-reading and understanding emotions as young as three years of age were, several years later, more likely to use reasoning in their disputes – rather than simply protesting or becoming overtly aggressive (A14). This points to the potential value of cognitive behavioural based approaches.

It is important to note that a lack of correlation has been demonstrated in children's conflict strategies between different relationships. Some children were able to use negotiation and reasoning with their mothers but not with their siblings and friends and vice versa. The dynamic and quality of particular relationships importantly affect the way children use their power of understanding to resolve or exacerbate conflict (A14).

Although there is a strong linear increase in the prevalence of non-aggressive antisocial behaviour from early childhood to late teenage years, physical aggression has been shown to decline as age increases from four years to adolescence. However, among some young people, the prevalence of serious physical aggression increases with age. Minor physical aggression appears to decline with age in the general population, but a small percentage of highly aggressive youths follow a different course (A18).

Aggression and violence are frequent causes of exclusion and children being taken into care. A systematic review (A34) examining school-based violence prevention programmes, which aimed to reduce aggression and violence in children from kindergarten to grade 12 (or international equivalent), found that such programmes may produce a modest reduction in aggressive and violent behaviours in children who already exhibit such behaviour. However, the authors noted that because of the many different interventions, controls and outcome measures included in the review, caution should be taken when interpreting the findings. (See also practice question 9, 'How can we help children and young people to stay in school?')

Direct observation in the home shows that much aggressive behaviour in children is influenced by the way parents behave toward them. Parents frequently do little to encourage polite or considerate behaviour by the child (B17) with the result that good and considerate behaviour is frequently ignored and bad behaviour gets attention.

A first step for managing aggressive behaviour is to ensure that parents receive support and have the requisite skills to successfully parent their child. Although there is sufficient research to support the provision of parent training for parents of young children (including the 2006 health technology assessment from NICE – A35), there is less research demonstrating its effectiveness for adolescents. An interesting development over recent years has been the provision of parenting programmes to parents of older children and young people with offending behaviours. A key change in the Youth Justice System in England and Wales over recent years has been the introduction of the Parenting Order, for parents of young people who are at risk of, or known to be, offending, or who do not attend school. To comply with the Parenting Order, parents must engage with parenting support and education services in a form directed by the court or their local youth offending team. An evaluation of the effectiveness of the Youth Justice Board's Parenting Programme which funded the development of 42 new parenting projects across England showed that most projects needed to adapt 'off-the-shelf' parenting courses for working with parents of young offenders (B19).

Despite initial aims to work with parents and their child with offending behaviour, as well as other family members, most projects only managed to work directly with the parents. Around 800 parents, 500 young people and 800 project workers provided information for the national evaluation of this programme. By the time parents left their projects they reported significant positive changes in parenting skills and competencies including:

- improved communication with their child
- reduction in the frequency of conflict with young people and better approaches to handling conflict
- better relationships, including more praise and approval for their child
- feeling better able to influence young people's behaviour (B19).

Interestingly the evaluation showed no difference in the level of benefit reported by parents who were referred voluntarily as opposed to being referred via a Parenting Order.

Project workers were generally less optimistic than parents about the benefits of the programme. However, when asked to provide a retrospective, overall judgement on how much each parent had benefited from the service, staff reported that nearly half (49 per cent) of parents had benefited substantially and only one in eight (12 per cent) had derived no benefit at all (B19).

There was some evidence that the young people's perceptions about their relationship with their parents had improved following the training, although this finding was frequently not found to be statistically significant. In the year after their parents left the parenting programme, reconviction rates of young people had reduced by approximately one third, offending behaviour that resulted in conviction had dropped to 56 per cent and the average number of offences per young person had dropped by 50 per cent. The authors caution that these improvements, although encouraging, are not likely to be the result of parenting programmes alone, which are unlikely to offer a quick fix for entrenched antisocial behaviour in young people (B19).

Aggressive children are thought to differ from non-aggressive children in their ability to process social information and for some children and young people this is thought to result in inappropriate behavioural responses. Programmes have therefore been developed to teach children and young people how to recognise and respond appropriately to social cues. The earliest programmes were developed in the 1970s and taught cognitive-based problem-solving skills. A recent systematic review (A56) explored the research that addressed school-based programmes of this type. The review identified 73 studies, and the authors concluded that students who participated in social information processing programmes with their classmates showed less aggressive and disruptive behaviour after treatment than those who did not participate. They noted that the programme had the potential to reduce the incidence of students in the USA who were getting into fights from 15 per cent to 8 per cent.

conclusions

Anger management, in combination with support for parents, shows potential for addressing less severe problems of aggression. Few studies specifically address the management of severe forms of aggression. Some school programmes aimed at reducing violence have been positively evaluated; see practice question 9, 'How can we help children and young people to stay in school?'

service examples

Brandon Centre, Camden Town, London

The Brandon Centre provides a self-referrring counselling and psychotherapy service for young people. Its principal objective is to maintain and develop an accessible and flexible professional service in response to the psychological, medical, sexual and social problems of young people aged 12 to 25 years.

The Brandon Centre aims to relieve distress, mobilise personal resources and facilitate growth in adolescents toward responsibility and self-fulfilment. It particularly aims to prevent or alleviate suffering caused by unwanted pregnancy, mental ill-health, psychological disturbance and maladaption in adult and future family relationships.

An evaluation of the service can be found on the website at: www.brandon-centre.org.uk/evaluation.php

Reframe Conduct Disorder Outreach Team, Newham, London

The outreach team works over a period of time with children and young people whose behaviour is very concerning and is making themselves and their parents or carers unhappy. The initiative demonstrates how to achieve high service take-up with marginalised families and has received a NIMH(E) Positive Practice Award.

For more information, go to: www.camhs.org.uk

question 9
how can we help children and young people to stay in school?

Unfortunately there is no easy answer to a question as complex as this. Children and young people truant from school for a wide variety of reasons, often to do with pressures at and in school. Sometimes this is a symptom of conduct disordered behaviour and needs to be considered as such. Messages can be drawn from research that explore the causes of school exclusion, initiatives to prevent school exclusion and also the views of children and young people who have been excluded.

The number of pupils excluded from school has been steadily increasing over recent years. The definition of exclusion from school is broad. It goes beyond definitions that tend to focus on school procedures and classroom management issues. Those who have disengaged with learning or are disaffected in any way are as effectively excluded as those who have been through the formal processes, whether or not they have drawn attention to their needs through behaviour problems. The excluded child often leaves school with little chance of re-entering mainstream education or training and the consequences on their future lives are far-reaching. Additional long-term implications include a drift toward juvenile crime, homelessness and dependency on welfare agencies (as in the case history of John described on p11).

A survey by the Audit Commission (B1) found that 42 per cent of young offenders had been excluded from school and a further 23 per cent 'truanted significantly'. The link between exclusion and crime has also been borne out in Home Office research, whose survey of self-reported offending found that almost all boys and nearly two-thirds of girls excluded from school admitted some type of offence (D15). While there is no proven causal link between exclusion from school and crime, it is reasonable to suppose that being in an unstructured environment increases the likelihood of offending, particularly when coupled with disaffection.

The Prince's Trust surveyed the opinions of almost 700 young people about key issues relating to race, school exclusion and leaving care. The results show that, for many young people excluded from school, their difficulty started at the point of transition from primary to secondary school. Many never came to terms with the size and anonymity of the secondary school, and the lack of apparent parental interest that most of them experienced left them without a key support when they needed it most (B31). Large class sizes and a lack of one-to-one attention from teachers meant these young people were unable to understand classroom tasks fully. Their educational and behavioural needs were not always detected or addressed, causing frustration, anger and further aggressive behaviour. Forty-two per cent of excluded pupils believed that no-one was encouraging them back to mainstream school. Compared to their non-excluded peers, they had a much lower rate of adult involvement in their lives (B31).

OFSTED's (Office for Standards in Education) report *Exclusions from Secondary Schools 1995/6* (D12) highlighted a variety of factors associated with poor behaviour, of which the most significant were: poor basic skills; limited aspirations and opportunities; family difficulties; poor relationships with other pupils, parents or teachers; and pressure from others to behave in a way that conflicted with authority. Other influential factors included the inability of parents or carers to exercise control, physical or sexual abuse, and racism.

There is a range of approaches that schools can take to reduce exclusions. These include initiatives to improve attendance, initiatives to tackle behaviour and wider initiatives to work closely with families and other relevant agencies. During 1999/2000, OFSTED undertook a series of ten inspections of secondary schools with a special focus on truancy and school exclusion (D13). Short visits were made to a further 80 secondary schools where truancy and exclusion rates were above the national average. Sixty-six per cent of permanent exclusions from secondary schools involved pupils aged 13 to 15, with 27 per cent involving 14-year-olds. The OFSTED inspections identified that schools that had improved attendance rates showed the following characteristics:

- A high degree of consistency in registration procedures, speedy analysis of attendance and systematic follow up of unexplained or inadequately excused absences.
- The provision of activities before and after school and specially tailored Key Stage 4 courses (not enough practical attempts are made to ensure that pupils who are absent from school catch up on the work they have missed).
- Education welfare services working constructively with schools on their policies and procedures, rather than exclusively on individual casework, and calling on the skills of education welfare officers in more complex cases.

Schools that had been able to demonstrate effective action on behaviour had:

- Clear expectations and routines, based on policies and procedures that are agreed, monitored and kept under review. (Most schools have explicit behaviour policies and sound guidance on how to exercise discipline, but, too often, lack of consistency in applying them allows some pupils to exploit situations and disrupt the experience of others.)

- Consistent use of rewards from Year 7 to Year 11 to encourage pupils to manage their behaviour. Consistency of approach helped pupils to perceive sanctions as reasonable.

Very few pupils are permanently excluded from school as a result of an isolated major incident. More usually, exclusion is the outcome of an accumulation of problems over time. Over half the schools inspected used a range of sanctions to avoid excluding pupils. Schools with a wide range of sanctions generally excluded fewer pupils.

School Restorative Conferencing (SRC) is another school-based approach to reduce exclusions. The remit of SRC is the inclusion and participation of children and young people in the decision-making process within school, with the aim of maintaining young people within the school community. SRC is derived from family restorative conferencing (also known as Family Group Conferencing) and applies the principles of restorative justice to young people at risk of exclusion from school.

The school restorative process is used frequently in the USA and Australia and research indicates that it can have a major impact on the reduction of school suspensions and exclusions and improvement in behaviour and relationships.

An evaluation of a pilot SRC study in Northern Ireland (B21) found:
- improved relationships between schools and families
- improved behaviour and attitudes in the child/young person
- allowing young people who had been excluded to return to the school system
- preventing young people who were at risk of suspension/expulsion from being excluded from school
- an increase in attendance rates
- an increase in performance levels
- a reduction in disruptive behaviour/bullying
- a reduction in suspension/exclusion
- an increase in young people remaining in the school system.

One approach to improve attendance and reduce exclusions is to promote good communication between the school and the family. An initiative specifically designed to improve communication between schools and families of pupils in 13 inner London schools (B20) has resulted in better attendance, improved punctuality and fewer fixed-term exclusions. The project was evaluated through face-to-face and telephone interviews, questionnaires, school reports and school and project documentation. The evaluation attributes the success of the project to factors including:
- the ability of project workers to respond to the individual needs of the schools in which they work
- joint management of the project (workers were accountable to the schools, but were trained and supervised by the project) and

- clarity about the role of the workers in the school, and workers being viewed both as part of the school and as 'different' – an important factor for both parents and pupils.

One three-year study (B2) examined the introduction of school social workers into a primary school and linked secondary school serving a deprived community with high rates of unemployment, crime and school exclusions. Compared to two control schools, the experimental school showed a significant reduction in rates of self-reported theft, truancy, bullying, hard drug use and exclusions, ie, behaviours associated with conduct disorder. The Behaviour and Education Support Teams (BESTs) (see practice question 7 'What is the current research on multidisciplinary involvement?') drew a number of agencies together around the school. (See box on p59 for a description of a service example of this in Manchester.)

Some groups of children and young people are more likely to be excluded than others. The permanent exclusion rate among children in care is ten times higher than the average and as many as 30 per cent of children in care are out of mainstream education through exclusion or truancy (D15). Although need among this group of young people has been identified, little research is available about potentially valuable interventions from an outcomes perspective. A number of factors have contributed to this situation (A44):

- frequent changes in placement
- mistrust of initiatives by the young people
- different use of language by health, social care and education
- historically poor data collection systems.

Reasons for the high level of exclusion include (A44):

- the absence of an adult to advocate consistently for them in contacts with education services
- poor concentration at school because of difficulties at home
- possible stigmatisation by pupils and teachers
- large gaps in schooling experienced by many young people while placements are being set up. (It has been reported that two out of three children who move to a foster home also change school, and that 80 per cent of looked after children whose placements break down, change school again. These moves lead to problems in coping with curriculum changes owing to the number of different schools attended) (O4).

One US report (C14) describes the impact of a manualised antiviolence programme on the learning climate in an elementary school over four years, compared with the outcome in a control school. The experimental school showed significant reductions in discipline referrals and increases in scores on standardised academic achievement measures.

A meta-analysis of small schools in the US (C5) shows that on many counts (eg, behaviour, parental involvement, truancy, drug abuse, pupil engagement), small schools were better than big schools. OFSTED also frequently reports better progress for pupils in small schools and the National Association of Small Schools holds information on this; go to www.smallschools.org.uk/#

Bearing this in mind, and the foregoing evidence, the practitioner needs to find the most nurturing educational environment for the conduct disordered young person.

conclusions

It is encouraging to find a range of initiatives and approaches that can address the cycle of truancy, school exclusion and antisocial behaviour. Providing structured support at points of transition in children's lives, ensuring consistent approaches toward behaviour, and actively involving children, young people and their parents in decision making are consistently highlighted as being important.

The implementation of the Healthy Schools Programme (D9) should increase the emphasis on children's emotional well-being in schools, and improved joint working between agencies is likely to ensure that the children's mental health needs are identified and addressed. The DfES publication, Promoting Children's Mental Health Within Early Years and School Settings, (D2) sets out some pointers for schools and identifies good practice examples.

ongoing research

Violence Reduction in Schools (VIRIS) is a project being carried out in joint partnership between UK Observatory for the Promotion of Non-Violence and DfES.

The first phase of this research has been completed and involved a detailed literature search to determine elements of good practice.

The research is in the second phase (2005) and is now concerned with the writing and production of training materials for VIRIS.

• further reading

Varnava G (2000) *Towards a Non-Violent Society: Checkpoints for Schools*. London: Forum on Children and Violence

Vernon J and Sinclair R (1998). *Maintaining Children in School: The contribution of social service departments*. London: National Children's Bureau

Fonagy P, Gergely G, Jurist E and Target M (2002) *Affect Regulation, Mentalization and the Development of the Self*. New York: Other Press service example

Manchester Behaviour and Education Support Teams

Manchester Local Education Authority has established four multiagency Behaviour and Education Support Teams (BESTs) to work across clusters of schools, consisting of a target secondary school and its main associated primaries, where there are high numbers of children with emotional and behavioural needs.

Protocols are in place so that the Behaviour Improvement Programme in Manchester Child and Adolescent Mental Health Services offers support and pupils can access specialist mental health services when needed.

The BESTs operate on a number of levels, supporting not only the needs of individual pupils and their families, but also the wider school community through group intervention work, staff training and surgeries, and emotional literacy programmes. Family work is a strong feature.

www.childrensnsfcasestudies.dh.gov.uk/children/nsfcasestudies.nsf

question 10
how can placement stability be enhanced?

There are over 76,000 children and young people in public care on any given day in the UK, approximately 50,000 (64 per cent) of whom live with 38,000 foster families (A55).

Stability and continuity of care are important protective factors for children and young people's health and well-being. Interviews with adults who had been raised in stable foster homes and had received specialist support from a dedicated foster agency found that 50 per cent of the respondents were 'well integrated socially' and 68 per cent were 'well integrated' or average (B14). By contrast, placements that were not stable resulted in discontinuity of the child's care, education and treatment for health problems. This indicates the need to ensure training and support for foster parents and an even greater need to keep some consistency in the child or young person's life if the placement breaks down (eg, same school, same social worker).

The historically high numbers of placement moves have reinforced concerns that the care system may be creating a sense of unpredictability that may obstruct the development of attachment in children. Factors contributing to success in improving placement stability are:

- thorough reviews of provision and needs analysis
- a wide range of partnerships
- a clear investment strategy
- a flexible approach to commissioning (A41).

Research suggests that three key factors are associated with placement breakdown:

1. the foster carers' confidence in their ability to handle problems
2. the severity of the child's mental health problems
3. the 'click' factor – the extent to which the 'chemistry' works between the foster parents and the children. Further research suggests that the click factor is largely influenced by the degree of disruptive behaviour in the child (A38).

Research has shown that the child's age at placement and a history of previous disruptions – but not the number of moves per se – predicted disruptions, as did emotional abuse, which had probably been experienced by almost half the children. A further predictor of poorer outcomes is children showing one of two kinds of insecure-attachment behaviour: aloofness (showing little affection and hiding emotions) or childish attachment (seeking attention through misbehaviour or indiscriminate friendliness). One study has identified that young people whom the foster carers felt had little or no attachment to an adult at the first interview, were more likely to have disruptive placements (A38). Behaviour problems have been shown to be one of the strongest predictors of a lack of success in placement. Challenging, overactive and restless behaviours were particularly implicated. However these difficulties may only lead to placement breakdown if they prompt the carers to reject the child (A38).

Approaches to enhance placement stability can be considered in three ways: through addressing the mental health needs of the individual child or young person; through providing support and training to foster carers; and through the provision of therapeutic foster care.

Children in care are much more likely to have experienced risk factors that predispose them to the development of mental disorders. The reasons for children being taken into care in 2005 included:

- abuse and neglect (49%)
- family dysfunction (13%)
- disability (3%)
- parental illness or disability (7%)
- family in acute stress (12%)
- socially unacceptable behaviour (6%)
- absent parenting (12%) (D5).

One UK study (B26) examined the prevalence and types of psychiatric disorder of all adolescents aged between 13 and 17 years in one local authority. It showed 96 per cent of adolescents in residential units and 57 per cent in foster care had psychiatric disorders. The prevalence of psychiatric disorders in a comparison group was 15 per cent. The most common diagnosis among adolescents was conduct disorder (28 per cent) followed by over-anxious disorder (26 per cent). Another study (B13) examined the mental health of children (mean age 9.6 years) at the time that they entered local authority care. The most common disorders among this group were conduct disorder and depression. Of the 70 children studied, 21 had severe attachment difficulties and 18 had autistic-like detachment.

A study of social workers' views about the mental health needs of a sample of foster children appeared to confirm this (B30). Here 80 per cent of the children were considered by social workers to require treatment from a mental health professional, but only 27 per cent had received any input.

Failure to acknowledge and treat mental health problems may lead to serious difficulties for these children ranging from an increase in placement breakdown to more serious mental health problems in later life (A43).

Although local authorities are required to monitor children's developmental progress and to ensure each looked after child has an annual medical report, there is substantial evidence that physical and mental health problems go unidentified and are inadequately managed. The uptake of health assessments in some local authorities is as low as 28 per cent (B8). Research by Ward (B37) found that parents in the community were more effective in accessing resources on their child's behalf than were local authorities on behalf of the children in their care.

One way that a fostering service can promote secure and caring relationships for children and young people is by providing a sustainable link between foster care and birth families. There is a presumption in the 1989 Children Act that, whenever practicable, contact with birth families is required. However recent research evidence suggests that contact requires very careful management and supervision to prevent any potential disruption to the young person's placement. Things that can help the management of contact include:

- paying attention to children's views of the importance of different family members and ensuring the child's welfare and safety during contact (in some circumstances and at certain points of time in their lives, children may not want to maintain links with all or some of their family)
- setting clear boundaries for contact, distinguishing between different family members for different purposes and contexts
- valuing the views of foster carers who are vital in helping children make sense of their family structure
- identifying and involving, where appropriate, other members of the young person's social support network who could provide care and attention (A55).

The provision of support and training for foster carers is seen as an important factor contributing to the successful outcome of foster care placements. Providing training for foster carers is thought to enhance caring attitudes and skills, help foster carers deal better with foster children's behaviour and decrease foster carer attrition (B10).

A Cochrane Review has evaluated the effectiveness of cognitive-behavioural training interventions for foster carers (A53) in improving a) looked after children's behavioural/relationship problems; b) foster carers' psychological well-being and functioning; c) foster family functioning; and d) foster agency outcomes. Only five trials met the inclusion criteria. The results from this review showed that training interventions had little effect on outcomes for looked after children, assessed in relation to psychological functioning, extent of behavioural problems and interpersonal functioning. Results relating to foster carer outcomes indicated some improvements in measures of behavioural management skills, attitudes and psychological functioning. There was no significant impact on foster agencies' outcomes. The authors found inconclusive evidence about the efficacy of cognitive behavioural therapy training interventions for foster carers.

A recent review of parenting support (A38) describes two studies that had undertaken research into fostering. The Supporting Fostering Study surveyed a large representative sample of 596 foster placements through questionnaires sent to social workers, carers and fostered children. There were, in addition, a small number of case studies of successful and unsuccessful placements. The Adolescent Fostering Study used interviews with foster carers, young people and social workers to look at the task of caring for 68 teenagers who had a history of emotional and behavioural difficulties and whose placements were intended to be long term. The following issues relating to fostering were identified:

- The most successful carers responded to and worked with young people's emotional age rather than their chronological age.
- Carers need initially to set limits that might be more liberal than would be the case with birth children and then gradually to make them more firm to get the young people used to boundaries. This process is contrary to the more usual parenting of teenagers, which involves a steady relaxation of control and acceptance of independence.
- One of the major differences between foster caring and birth parenting is the concept of commitment of foster carers to the children and vice versa. Birth parents and children seldom think seriously about ending their relationship or denying their obligations and attachment to each other.
- Both studies show that there are fewer disruptions in the face of emotional and behavioural problems if the carers get some reward from the child's positive feelings for them.
- Responsiveness, commitment and a good working relationship between foster carers and social workers can contain challenging behaviour but the task remains formidable. Any additional stresses within or outside the household can destabilise the situation, and once negative spirals develop, the likelihood of success is low.
- Short breaks for carers did not improve outcomes. If anything the association was in the opposite direction, ie, breaks were associated with poorer outcomes. (This is, of course, almost certainly because breaks were a marker of more problems, especially antisocial behaviour in adolescence; they may also give a negative message to the child about the security of the main placement.)

Research carried out in York showed that support from social workers, family placement social workers, other foster carers or children's services was not associated with more successful placements. Specialist mental health input was linked to poor outcomes, probably because it was triggered by a worsening situation rather than actually causing it. There were two exceptions to this rule: aggressive children who received special help using a behavioural approach were said by carers to become less aggressive; and children who had seen an educational psychologist were less likely to have a placement breakdown. This was perhaps either because this improved school attendance or because referrals to educational psychologists were more likely if everyone was determined to keep the child in the placement (A38).

This York study was included as one of 16 studies of fostering examined in 2005 (D14) to extract the cumulative evidence. Successful placements were more likely to occur where:

- young people were receiving counselling
- social workers arranged services for the young people
- foster carers were supported by their immediate family, or received 'useful' support from their social networks or from local professionals (support from their parents and children was particularly crucial for lone carers)
- foster carers received useful support from the young people's social workers.

This review also found evidence to suggest that the usual levels of contact with mental health professionals do not affect outcomes, with the only possible exceptions of counselling and educational psychology.

Local strategies need to promote recruitment and retention of foster carers. Successful recruitment practice based on word-of-mouth, small cash incentives and targeted schemes appear to work best for the recruitment of foster carers. The involvement of foster carers in recruitment campaigns has also been shown to have a positive impact on recruitment (A50).

Research studies highlight the importance of the following factors in foster carer retention:

- frequent contact with social workers
- feeling treated as a colleague
- guaranteed respite care
- the availability of out-of-hours telephone help lines
- well-managed payment schemes
- higher than average levels of pay
- early access to specialist help and advice
- opportunities for taking part in training with other foster carers as a means of developing informal social support networks (A50, A55).

Many young people describe a sense of security when living with their extended family which comes from the love, belonging and sense of identity they receive (B6). Kinship care may not be the right choice for all children and research is equivocal about some of its potential benefits (A55). For example, while some studies report that children placed with kinship carers experience fewer psychological problems, other studies suggest that children are more likely to experience further abuse or neglect.

A new **research in practice** research review, due for publication in 2007, indicates that levels of stability in kinship care placements are as good – and often better – than in non-kin foster care placements. Children in kinship care, however, are more likely to live in poverty, with their carers less likely to receive support from children's services. (Nixon P, due for publication in 2007: www.rip.org.uk/publications).

Therapeutic foster care, also known as treatment foster care, wrap-around foster care and multidimensional foster care, provides the environment and support to address serious levels of emotional, behavioural or physical health problems. It may involve the provision of intensive support to the children or young people and their biological family (A50), the provision of training to birth parents and intensive work to address challenging behaviours with the individual child or young person. It generally aims to change the negative trajectory of antisocial behaviour by improving social adjustment with family members and peers through simultaneous and well co-ordinated treatments in the home, school and community. Treatment is provided in a family setting where new skills can be practised and reinforced.

Therapeutic foster care schemes are marked by a number of features:
· an above-average level of support, training and remuneration of carers
· a co-ordinated method of working that aims to treat behaviours in home, school and community
· clinical staff, including psychiatrists that support the placement
· a specified length of stay (A55).

Existing treatment foster care programmes, such as that pioneered at the Maudsley Hospital and Coram Family (B4) in London, suggest positive outcomes in terms of placement stability and education in particular. The Department for Education and Skills is currently funding an £11 million pilot programme of treatment foster care. Ten local authorities have been funded to introduce Treatment Foster Care: Cheshire; Dudley; Durham; Kent; Solihull; Southampton; Surrey; Wandsworth; Wirral; and Bournemouth, Dorset and Poole working together. Training is being provided centrally by the South London and Maudsley Trust and will include on-site supervision for local social workers, foster carers and clinical teams.

There are also developments in shared parenting (more often known as respite care) where a family is recruited to support another specific vulnerable family, taking over the parenting when, for example, a parent needs hospitalisation.

conclusions

This is an area where research is able to highlight areas for action. Addressing the needs of foster carers and providing adequate mental health services for children and young people are likely to lead to a reduction in placement moves. A final and vitally important feature to improve placement stability is ensuring that sufficient attention is paid to the children's placement choices (interviews with children have shown the importance of allowing them to be involved in decision-making regarding placements).

ongoing research

Enhancing Placement Stability is a randomised controlled trial of the effectiveness and comparative costs of standard social work services compared with two specific interventions designed to enhance adoptive parenting. The study includes 180 adoptive families with recently placed children aged 3 to 8 years who are showing signs of disturbed behaviour.

The randomised controlled trial, funded by the Nuffield Foundation and the Department of Health, will not be finished until 2007, but there is an initial paper: Rushton A, Monck E, Upright H and Davidson M (2006) 'Enhancing adoptive parenting: devising promising interventions' Child and Adolescent Mental Health, 11 (1).

• further reading

Social Exclusion Unit (2003) *"A Better Education for Children in Care"* (This is a good practice guide produced by the Social Exclusion Unit to support local authorities in improving education for children in care.) Available online at: www.socialexclusionunit.gov.uk/publications.asp?did=189
The Fostering Network and Department for Education and Skills (2004) *Good Practice Guidelines on the Recruitment of Foster Carers*. London: DfES

service examples

Liverpool Rosta Project

This a therapeutic fostering project with wrap-around mental health support serving 12- to 17-year-old looked after children with complex needs. An interagency, multidisciplinary team provides therapeutic foster care with intensive support and clinical supervision, individual and family therapy, systemic consultation, individual and group-based day programme, educational re-integration, psychiatric consultation and a 24-hour support worker service.
www.youngminds.org.uk/innovationprojects/liverpool.php

Leicester Respite Care Service

This service provides a series of pre-planned short-term placements of a particular child with the same carer. The length and timing of the arrangements can vary according to the specific needs of the child

and their family.
www.leicester.gov.uk/index.asp?pgid=16455

appendix 1
glossary and abbreviations

ADHD Attention Deficit Hyperactivity Disorder (ADHD) is a condition where there is increased motor activity in association with poor attention span.

bias An unintentional influence or effect which may occur at any stage of the research process and which distorts the findings.

children in special circumstances This refers to those children and young people for whom access to services has often been a particular problem. These are often the children who require a high degree of co-operation between staff in different agencies but who are also at most risk of achieving poorer outcomes than their peers. They tend to be 'lost' between agencies and are therefore not in receipt of services, even those that are provided universally.

Cochrane Review Systematic review published in the Cochrane Database of Systematic Reviews which is part of the Cochrane Library.

cognitive behavioural (programmes/therapy) A broad range of therapies with a common theme of combining approaches to address thoughts and their interactions with behaviour and emotions. Therapies are usually highly structured and relatively brief (6 – 24 sessions).

cohort study Involves identification of two groups (cohorts) of patients, one which received the exposure of interest and one which did not, and following these cohorts forward for the outcome of interest.

community (or full service) schools The provision on school premises of easily accessible family and community services such as child care, study support, police, health and social services, breakfast clubs, after school clubs and adult, family and community learning.

conduct disorder Behaviours characterised by a repetitive and persistent pattern of antisocial, aggressive or defiant behaviour.

controls In a randomised controlled trial (RCT), controls refer to the participants in the comparison group. They are allocated either to placebo, no treatment or a standard treatment.

co-morbidity More than one medical/psychiatric condition present.

Connexions Connexions is the government's support service for all young people aged 13 to 19. It aims to provide advice, guidance and access to personal development opportunities for this age group and to help them make a smooth transition to adulthood and working life.

CRD (Centre for Reviews and Dissemination) aims to provide research-based information about the effects of interventions used in health and social care. It helps to promote the use of research-based knowledge, by offering:

- rigorous and systematic reviews of research on selected topics
- scoping reviews which map the research literature
- three databases: DARE, NHS EED and HTA
- a dissemination service
- an information and enquiry service

demonstration project A project where more ideal conditions exist than are found in routine practice. For example: subjects may be selected to exclude those with complex problems; highly trained and/or motivated staff may be involved to deliver the intervention; or the level of supervision may exceed normal conditions.

emotional disorders The term emotional disorder is used to describe depressive, obsessive, hysterical, phobic or anxious disorders in children and young people. Often the clinical picture is mixed.

empirical research Experimental research.

epidemiological studies Research which studies the incidence and distribution of diseases and their control and prevention.

extended school Extended schools provide a range of services and activities, often beyond the school day, to help meet the needs of pupils, their families and the wider community.

Healthy Schools A joint Department for Education and Skills (DfES) and Department of Health (DH) funded programme. The overall aim is to help schools become healthy and effective in providing an environment that is conducive to learning and that encourages pupils to achieve. Core components of the Healthy Schools Programme are healthy eating; physical activity; comprehensive personal, social and health education (PSHE) and emotional well-being. Each local programme has a local co-ordinator and a team from education and health supporting its management and delivery.

health promotion Includes the provision of information about healthier lifestyles and how to make the best use of health services, with the intention of enabling people to make rational choices and of ensuring awareness of the factors of determining the health of the community.

Healthy Start Government scheme to provide advice on healthy living and financial help to pregnant women and young children in low-income families to buy a range of healthy foods. Replaces the Welfare Food Scheme.

internalising disorders Disorders such as anxiety and depression.

longitudinal study A study by which the same subjects are studied at different points over a period of time.

looked after children Under the Children Act 1989, a child is defined as being looked after by a local authority if he or she is in their care or is provided with accommodation for more than 24 hours by the authority.

meta-analysis A statistical technique that summarises the results of several studies in a single weighted estimate. More weight is given to studies with more events or sometimes to studies of higher quality.

MST See multi-systemic therapy

multidimensional foster care Also called Multidimensional Treatment Foster Care (MTFC) and Treatment Foster Care - the MTFC programme developed in the USA by the Oregon Social Learning Center, provides a wrap-around, multilevel intervention for young people, to help them in all areas of their life including the development of better attachment relationships and life skills.

multilevel interventions Interventions aimed at more than one dimension of a young person's life. For example, interventions may occur with families, at school, and on an individual basis.

multimodal interventions A range of methods and types of intervention may be required. For example, parent training, CBT for the young person, and additional support and training for teachers.

multisystemic therapy (MST) a highly intensive approach that involves the whole family and uses family strengths to improve relations, peer relations and school performance.

NeLH (National Electronic Library for Health) provides a single source of health information for health professionals but it can also be used by the general public. It provides links to national agencies, access to a wide range of expert knowledge and a wealth of information in its specialist libraries. See www.nelh.nhs.uk

NCB The National Children's Bureau is a charitable organisation that promotes the interests and well-being of all children and young people across every aspect of their lives.

NICE The National Institute for Health and Clinical Excellence is a special health authority for England and Wales. Its role is to provide patients, health professionals and the public with authoritative, robust and reliable guidance on current 'best practice'. See www.nice.org.uk

parenting order Parenting Orders can be given to the parents/carers of young people who offend, truant or who have received a Child Safety Order, Antisocial Behaviour Order or Sex Offender Order. It lasts for three months, but can be extended to 12 months. A parent/carer who receives a Parenting Order will be required to attend counselling or guidance sessions. They may also have conditions imposed on them such as attending their child's school, ensuring their child does not visit a particular place unsupervised or ensuring their child is at home at particular times. A failure to fulfil the conditions can be treated as a criminal offence and the parent/carer can be prosecuted.

pragmatic study Research designed to provide results that are directly applicable to normal practice.

prevalence The proportion of people with a finding, or disease, in a given population at a given time.

problem-solving skills training This form of training helps children and young people to develop interpersonal cognitive problem-solving skills. It is an individual treatment usually carried out in 20 sessions.

quasi-randomised controlled trial A trial using a method of allocating participants to different forms of care that are not truly random. For example, by date of birth, medical record number or the order in which participants are enrolled in the study.

randomised controlled trial (RCT) A trial in which participants are randomly assigned to two or more groups: at least one (the experimental group) receiving an intervention that is being tested and the other (control or comparison group) receiving an alternative treatment.

RCT See randomised controlled trial.

statistically significant The findings of a study that are unlikely to have arisen by chance.

systematic review A review in which a predefined methodology is used to identify, appraise and summarise studies that address a defined question.

Sure Start Part of the government's drive to tackle child poverty, Sure Start local programmes and children's centres are concentrated in areas where a high proportion of children are living in poverty. Sure Start works with parents and parents-to-be to improve children's life chances through:

• family support

• advice on nurturing

• health services

• early learning.

Sure Start Plus A pilot programme running in 35 local authorities until 2006. Sure Start Plus aims to reduce the risk of long-term social exclusion resulting from teenage pregnancy, through co-ordinated support to pregnant teenagers and teenage parents under 18.

YOT Youth Offending Teams bring together local key agencies with a contribution to make to reduce offending by children and young people.

references – classified

References are grouped according to the nature of the source material, as well as in a more traditional alphabetical listing by author. They are classified into the following categories:

A Secondary research or reviews

B Primary research or evaluations conducted in the UK

C Primary research or evaluations conducted outside the UK

D Policy and official publications

0 Other

Within each group the references have a consecutive number. **research in practice** has adopted this method as a quick way for readers to identify the type of evidence and to find references with minimal disruption to the flow of text.

A Secondary research or reviews

A1
Alexander J, Barton C and Deal G (2005) 'Functional Family Therapy' in *Blueprints for Violence Prevention*, Book 3. Boulder, CO: Centre for the Study and Prevention of Violence

A2
Bailey S (2000) 'Serious Antisocial Behaviour' in Aggleton P, Hurry J and Warwick I (eds) *Young People and Mental Health*. Chichester: John Wiley and Sons

A3
Barlow J and Parsons J (2003) 'Group Based Parent-training Programmes for Improving Emotional and Behavioural Adjustment in 0-3 Year Old Children' *The Cochrane Database of Systematic Reviews* (2) CD003680 Oxford: Update Software

A4
Barlow J (1997) *Systematic Review of the Effectiveness of Parent-training Programmes in Improving Behavioural Problems in Children Aged 3-10 Years: A review of the literature on parent-training programmes and child behaviour outcome measures.* Oxford: Update Software

A5
Benson BA and Havercamp SM (2004) 'Behavioural Approaches to Treatment: Principles and practices' in Bouras N (ed), *Psychiatric and Behavioural Disorders in Developmental Disabilities and Mental Retardation.* Cambridge: Cambridge University Press

A6
Cameron A, Lart R, Harrison L, Macdonald G and Smith R (2000) *Factors Promoting and Obstacles Hindering Joint Working: A systematic review.* Bristol: School for Policy Studies, University of Bristol

A7
Canning U, Millward L, Raj T and Warm D (2004) *Drug Use Prevention Among Young People: A review of reviews.* London: Health Development Agency

A8
Chadwick O, Taylor E and Bernard S (1998) *The Prevention of Behaviour Disorders in Children with Severe Learning Disability.* Final Report to the NHS Executive. London: Institute of Psychiatry

A9
Chamberlain P and Rosicky JG (1995) 'The Effectiveness of Family Therapy in the Treatment of Adolescents with Conduct Disorder and Delinquency' *Journal of Marital and Family Therapy* (21)

A10
Children's Mental Health Ontario (2001) *Children and Adolescents with Conduct Disorder: Findings from the literature and clinical consultation in Ontario.* Online version available at: www.cmho.org (checked 5 December 2006)

A11
Deklyen M and Speltz ML (2001) 'Attachment and Conduct Disorder' in Hill J and Maughan B (eds) *Conduct Disorders in Childhood and Adolescence.* Cambridge: Cambridge University Press

A12
Dodge K, Dishion T and Lansford J (2006) *Deviant Peer Influences in Intervention and Public Policy for Youth.* Washington: Society for Research in Child Development

A13
Dryfoos JG (1990) *Adolescents at Risk: Prevalence and prevention.* New York: Oxford University Press (USA)

A14
Dunn J (2001) 'Development of Prosocial Behaviour and Conflict' in Hill J and Maughan B (eds) *Conduct Disorders in Childhood and Adolescence.* Cambridge: Cambridge University Press

A15
Evans J, Harden A, Thomas J and Benefield P (2003) *Support for Pupils with Emotional and Behavioural Difficulties (EBD) in Mainstream Primary School Classrooms: A systematic review of the effectiveness of interventions.* London: Evidence for Policy and Practice Information and Co-ordinating Centre (EPPI-Centre) and the National Foundation for Educational Research (NFER)

A16
Farrington DP (1999) 'Conduct Disorder and Deliquency' in Steinhausen HC and Verhulst FC (eds) *Risks and Outcomes in Developmental Psychopathology.* Oxford: Oxford University Press

A17
Flouri E (2005) *Fathering and Child Outcomes.* Chichester: Wiley

A18
Fonagy P and Kurtz A (2002) 'Disturbance of Conduct' in Fonagy P, Target M, Cottrell D, Phillips J and Kurtz Z (eds) *What Works for Whom? A Critical Review of Treatments for Children and Adolescents.* New York: Guilford Press

A19
Fonagy P and Roth A (eds) (2004) *What Works For Whom? A Critical Review of Psychotherapy Research (Second Edition)* New York: Guilford Press

A20

Foxcroft D, Ireland D, Lister-Sharp D and Breen R (2002) 'Primary Prevention for Alcohol Misuse in Young People' *The Cochrane Database of Systematic Reviews* (3)

A21

Hassiotis A and Hall I (2004) 'Behavioural and Cognitive-behavioural Interventions for Outwardly-directed Aggresssive Behaviour in People with Learning Disabilities' *The Cochrane Database of Systematic Reviews*, (1)

A22

Henggler S, Schoenwald S, Borduin C, Rowland MD and Cunningham PB (1998) *Multisystemic Treatment of Antisocial Behaviour in Children and Adolescents.* New York: Guilford Press

A23

Hill J and Maughan B (eds) (2001) *Conduct Disorders in Childhood and Adolescence.* Cambridge: Cambridge University Press

A24

Hinde RA (2001) 'Can the study of "normal" behaviour contribute to an understanding of conduct disorder?' in Hill J and Maughan B (eds) *Conduct Disorders in Childhood and Adolescence.* Cambridge: Cambridge University Press

A25

Kazdin AE (1997) 'Practitioner Review: Psychological treatments for conduct disorder in children' *Journal of Child Psychology and Psychiatry* 38 (2)

A26

Keenan K, Loeber R and Green S (1999) 'Conduct Disorder in Girls: A Review of the Literature' *Clinical Child and Family Psychology Review* 2 (1) March 1999

A27

Kennedy E (2004) *Child and Adolescent Psychotherapy: A systematic review of psychoanalytic approaches.* London: North Central London Strategic Health Authority

A28

Liabo K (2002) 'Cognitive Behavioural Therapy for Young Offenders' *Evidence Nugget. What Works for Children?* London: City University

A29

Linck P, Parry-Jones B, Elliston P, Miles L and Robinson CA (2001) *The Inter-agency Working Capabilities of Local Health Groups.* Bangor: Institute of Medical and Social Care Research, University of Wales

A30

Littell JH, Popa M and Forsythe B (2005) 'Multisystemic Therapy for social, emotional, and behavioral problems in youth aged 10-17' *The Cochrane Database of Systematic Reviews* (4) CD004797. DOI: 10.1002/14651858.CD004797.pub4

A31

Loeber R and Coie J (2001) 'Continuities and Discontinuities of Development, with Particular Emphasis on Emotional and Cognitive Components of Disruptive Behaviour' in Hill J and Maughan B (eds) *Conduct Disorders in Childhood and Adolescence.* Cambridge: Cambridge University Press

A32

Lyne P, Allen D and Satherley P (2001) *Systematic Review of Evidence of Effective Methods for Removing Barriers to Change to Improve Collaborative Working.* Bangor: Institute for Medical and Social Care Research, University of Wales

A33

Montgomery P, Bjornstad G and Dennis J (2006) 'Media-based behavioural treatments for behavioural problems in children' *The Cochrane Database of Systematic Reviews* (1) CD002206. DOI: 10.1002/14651858.CD002206.pub3

A34

Mytton JA, Di Guiseppi C, Gough DA, Taylor R and Logan S (2002) School-based Violence Prevention Programmes: Systematic review of secondary prevention trials. *Archives of Pediatrics and Adolescent Medicine 156*

A35

National Institute for Health and Clinical Excellence (2006) *Parent-training/education Programmes in the Management of Children with Conduct Disorders.* London: NICE. Online version available at: www.nice.org.uk/page.aspx?o=TA102 (checked 5 December 2006)

A36

Oeklyen M and Speltz ML (2001) 'Attachment and conduct disorder' in Hill J and Maughan B (eds) *Conduct Disorders in Childhood and Adolescence.* Cambridge: Cambridge University Press

A37

Offord D and Bennett K (1994) 'Conduct Disorder: Long term outcomes and intervention effectiveness' *Journal of the American Academy of Child and Adolescent Psychiatry 33*

A38

Quinton D (2004) *Supporting Parents: Messages from research.* London: Jessica Kingsley

A39

Qureshi H (1993) 'Impact on Families: Young adults with learning disability who show challenging behaviour', in Kleinan C (ed) *Research to Practice? Implications of research on the challenging behaviour of people with learning disability.* Kidderminster: BILD

A40

Reese RM, Hellings JA and Schroeder SR (2004) 'Treatment Methods for Destructive and Aggressive Behaviour in People with Severe Mental Retardation/Developmental Disabilities' in Bouras N (ed) *Psychiatric and Behavioural Disorders in Developmental Disabilities and Mental Retardation.* Cambridge: Cambridge University Press

A41

Richardson J (2002) *The Mental Health of Looked After Children.* London: The Mental Health Foundation

A42

Richardson J and Joughin C (2002a) *Parent Training Programmes for the Management of Young Children with Conduct Disorder.* London: Gaskell

A43

Richardson J and Joughin C (2002b) *The Mental Health Needs of Looked After Children.* London: Gaskell

A44
Richardson J and Lelliott P (2003) 'Mental Health of Looked After Children' *Advances in Psychiatric Treatment* 9

A45
Roberts H, Liabo K, Lucas P, DuBois D and Sheldon T (2004) 'Mentoring to reduce antisocial behaviour in childhood' *British Medical Journal* 328 28 February

A46
Rutter M (1999) 'Resilience Concepts and Findings: Implications for family therapy' *Journal of Family Therapy* 21

A47
Rutter M, Giller A and Hagell A (1998) *Antisocial Behaviour by Young People.* Cambridge: Cambridge University Press

A48
Sanders M, Gooley S and Nicholson J (2000) 'Early Intervention in Conduct Problems in Children' in Kosky R, O'Hanlon A, Martin G and Davis C (eds) *Clinical Approaches to Early Interventions in Child and Adolescent Mental Health (3)* Adelaide: The Australian Early Intervention Network for Mental Health in Young People

A49
Sebba J and Sachdvev D (1997) *What Works in Inclusive Education.* Barkingside: Barnardo's

A50
Sellick C and Howell D (2003) *Innovative, Tried and Tested: A review of good practice in fostering. Knowledge Review 4.* London: Social Care Institute for Excellence

A51
Stewart-Brown S, Fletcher L, Wadsworth M and Shaw R (2002) *The Roots of Social Capital II: A systematic review of longitudinal studies linking relationships in the home with health and disease.* Oxford: Health Services Research Unit, University of Oxford

A52
Tonge B (2004) 'Psychopathology of Children with Developmental Disabilities' in Bouras N *Psychiatric and Behavioural Disorders in Developmental Disabilities and Mental Retardation.* Cambridge: Cambridge University Press

A53   -
Turner W, Macdonald GM and Dennis JA (2005) 'Cognitive Behavioural Training Interventions for Assisting Foster Carers in the Management of Difficult Behaviour' *The Cochrane Database of Systematic Reviews 2.* Oxford: Update Software

A54
Waller S, Naidoo B and Thom B (2002) *The Prevention and Reduction of Alcohol Misuse.* London: Health Development Agency

A55
Wilson K, Sinclair I, Taylor C, Pithouse A and Sellick C (2004) *Fostering Success: An exploration of the research literature in foster care. Knowledge Review 5.* London: Social Care Institute for Excellence

A56

Wilson SJ and Lipsey MW (2006) *School-based Social Information Processing Interventions and Aggressive Behaviour for Universal Programmes (Part 1)*. Campbell Collaboration systematic review. Available online at www.campbellcollaboration.org (checked 5 December 2006)

A57

Wilson SJ, Lipsey MW and Derzon JH (2002) 'The Effects of School-based Intervention Programs on Aggressive and Disruptive Behaviour: A meta-analysis' *Journal of Consulting and Clinical Psychology*

A58

Wolpert M, Fuggle P and Cottrell D (2002) *Drawing on the Evidence*. Leicester: The British Psychological Society

A59

Woolfenden SR, Williams K and Peat J (2001) 'Family and Parenting Interventions in Children and Adolescents with Conduct Disorder and Delinquency Aged 10-17' in *The Cochrane Database of Systematic Reviews* Oxford: Update Software

B Primary research or evaluations conducted in the UK

B1

Audit Commission (1996) *Misspent Youth*. London: Audit Commission.

B2

Bagley C and Pritchard (1998) 'The Reduction of Problem Behaviours and School Exclusions in at-risk Youth: An experimental study of school social work with cost benefit analysis'. *Child and Family Social Work*, 3

B3

Ball M (2002) *Intervening Early*. London: Department for Education and Skills

B4

Brady L, Harwin J, Pugh G, Scott J and Sinclair R (2005) *Specialist Fostering for Young People with Challenging Behaviour*. London: Coram Family

B5

Broad B (ed) (2001) *Kinship Care: The placement choice for children and young people*. Lyme Regis: Russell House

B6

Broad B, Hayes R and Rushforth C (2001) *Kith and Kin: Kinship care for vulnerable young people*. York: Joseph Rowntree Foundation/National Children's Bureau

B7

Buchanan A, Hunt J, Bretherton H and Bream V (2002) *Families in Conflict: Perspectives of children and parents on the Family Court Welfare System*. Bristol: Bristol Policy Press

B8

Butler I and Payne H (1997) 'The Health of Children Looked After by the Local Authority' *Adoption and Fostering* 21

B9

Callaghan J, Pace F, Young B and Vostanis P (2003) 'Primary Mental Health Workers within Youth Offending Teams: A new service model' *Journal of Adolescence* 26

B10
Chamberlain P, Moreland S and Reid K (1992) 'Enhanced Services and Stipends for Foster Parents: Effects on retention rates and outcomes for children' *Child Welfare* 71 (5)

B11
Collishaw S, Maughan B and Goodman R (2004) 'Time trends in adolescent mental health'. *Journal of Child Psychology and Psychiatry*, 45 (8)

B12
Cowie H, Naylor P, Talamelli L, Chauhan P and Smith PK (2002) 'Knowledge, use of and attitudes towards peer support' *Journal of Adolescence* 25 (5)

B13
Dimigen G, Del Priore C and Butler S (1999) 'Psychiatric Disorder Among Children at Time of Entering Local Authority Care: Questionnaire survey' *British Medical Journal* 319

B14
Dumaret AC, Coppel-Batsh M and Couraud S (1997) 'Adult Outcomes of Children Reared for Long Time Periods in Foster Families' *Child Abuse and Neglect* 21

B15
Farrington DP (1995) 'The Development of Offending and Antisocial Behaviour from Childhood: Key findings from the Cambridge study in delinquent development' *Journal of Child Psychology and Psychiatry and Allied Disciplines* 360

B16
Ferri E and Smith K (2005) *Step Parenting in the 1990s*. London: Family Policies Studies Centre

B17
Gardner EM (1992) 'Parent-child Interaction and Conduct Disorder' *Educational Psychology Review* 4 (2)

B18
Gesch CB, Hammond SM, Hampson SE, Eves A and Crowder MJ (2002) 'Influence of supplementary vitamins, minerals and essential fatty acids on the antisocial behaviour of young adult prisoners' *British Journal of Psychiatry* 181

B19
Ghate D and Ramella M (2002) *A National Evaluation of the Youth Justice Board's Parenting Programme*. London: Policy Research Bureau

B20
Hallam S and Castle F (1999) *Evaluation of a School-Home Liaison Project – London Diocesan Board for Schools*. London: Institute of Education, University of London

B21
Healy J, Gribben M and McCann C (2005) *School Restorative Conferencing. No 4 Policy and Practice Briefing*. Northern Ireland: Barnardo's. Available online at www.barnardos.org.uk (checked 17 October 2006)

B22
Jaffee SR and Caspi A (2001) 'Predicting Early Fatherhood and Whether Young Fathers Live with Their Children' *Journal of Child Psychology and Psychiatry*, 42 (6)

B23
Kearney P, Levin E and Rosen G (2000) *Alcohol, Drug and Mental Health Problems: Working with families.* London: National Institute of Social Work

B24
Lloyd G, Stead J and Kendrick A (2001) *Hanging on in There: A study of interagency work to prevent school exclusion in three local authorities.* London: National Children's Bureau

B25
Lloyd N, O'Brien M and Lewis C (2003) *Fathers in Sure Start Local Programmes.* Nottingham: DfES Publications

B26
McCann JB, James A and Wilson S (1996) 'Prevalence of Psychiatric Disorders in Young People in the Care System' *British Medical Journal* 313

B27
Meltzer H, Green H, McGinnity A, Ford T and Goodman R (2005) *Mental Health of Children and Young People in Great Britain, 2004.* London: Office for National Statistics

B28
The Mental Health Foundation (2004) *Effective Joint Working Between CAMHS and Schools.* Research Report 412. London: Department for Education and Skills

B29
Osler A, Street C, Lall M and Vincent K (2001) *Not a Problem? Girls and exclusion from school.* London: National Children's Bureau/Joseph Rowntree Foundation

B30
Phillips J (1997) 'Meeting the Psychiatric Needs of Children in Foster Care: Social workers' views' *Psychiatric Bulletin* 21

B31
The Prince's Trust (2002) *The Way It Is: Young people on race, school exclusion and leaving care.* London: The Prince's Trust

B32
Pringle A (2004) 'Can Watching Football be a Component of Developing a State of Mental Health for Men?' *The Journal of the Royal Society for the Promotion of Health* 124 (3)

B33
St. James-Roberts I, Greenlaw G, Simon A and Hurry J (2005) *National Evaluation of Youth Justice Board Mentoring Schemes 2001-2004.* London: Youth Justice Board

B34
Scott S (2004) 'Parent Training Programmes' in Rutter M and Taylor E (eds) *Child and Adolescent Psychiatry.* Oxford: Blackwell Science

B35
Social Exclusion Unit & The Who Cares? Trust (2002) *Report on Education of Children and Young People in Care.* London: Social Exclusion Unit

B36
Vernon J and Sinclair R (1998) *Maintaining Children in School: The contribution of social service departments.* London: National Children's Bureau

B37
Ward H (1995) *Looking After Children: Research into practice.* London: The Stationery Office

B38
Welsh E, Buchanan A, Flouri E and Lewis J (2005) *'Involved' Fathering and Child Well-being: Fathers' involvement with secondary school children*. London: National Children's Bureau

C Primary research or evaluations conducted outside the UK

C1
Armbruster P and Kazdin AE (1994) 'Attrition in Child Psychotherapy' *Advances in Clinical Child Psychology* 16

C2
Brinker RP, Seifer R and Sameroff AJ (1994) 'Relations Among Maternal Stress, Cognitive Development and Early Intervention in Middle and Low SES Infants with Developmental Disabilities' *American Journal on Mental Retardation* (4)

C3
Brown SA, D'Amico EJ, McCarthy DM and Tapert SF (2001) 'Four-year outcomes from adolescent alcohol and drug treatment' *Journal of Studies on Alcohol* (62) 3

C4
Cote S, Tremblay R, Nagin D, Zoccolillo M and Vitaro F (2002) 'Childhood Behavioral Profiles Leading to Adolescent Conduct Disorder: Risk trajectories for boys and girls' *Journal of the American Academy of Child & Adolescent Psychiatry* 41 (9)

C5
Cotton K (1996) *School Size, School Climate and Student Performance*, School Improvement Research Series. Online version available at www.nwrel.org/scpd/sirs/10/c020.html (checked 5 December 2006)

C6
Grella CE, Hser YI, Joshi V and Rounds-Bryant J (2001) 'Drug Treatment Outcomes for Adolescents with Co-morbid Mental and Substance Use Disorders' *The Journal of Nervous and Mental Disease* 189

C7
Holland R, Moretti MM, Verlaan V and Peterson S (1993) 'Attachment and Conduct Disorder: The Response Programme' *Canadian Journal of Psychiatry* 38

C8
McCabe K, Lansing A, Garland A and Hough R (2002) 'Gender Differences in Psychopathology, Functional Impairment, and Familial Risk Factors Among Adjudicated Delinquents' *Journal of American Academy of Child and Adolescent Psychiatry* 41

C9
Moffitt TE (2003) 'Life-course-persistent and Adolescent-limited Antisocial Behavior' in Lahey B, Moffitt T and Caspi A (eds) *Causes of Conduct Disorder and Juvenile Delinquency*. New York: The Guildford Press

C10
Moffitt T, Caspi A, Rutter M and Silva P (2001) *Sex Differences in Antisocial Behaviour: Conduct disorder, delinquency and violence in the Dunedin longitudinal study*. Cambridge: Cambridge University Press

C11
Molgaard VK, Spoth RL and Redmond C (2000) *Competency Training: The strengthening families program for parents and youth 10-14.* Washington DC: Office of Juvenile Justice and Deliquency Prevention

C12
Quinn J (1995) 'Positive Effects of Participations in Youth Organizations' in Rutter M (ed) *Psychological Disturbances in Young People: Challenges for prevention.* Cambridge, New York, Melbourne: Cambridge University Press

C13
Shoham VI, Davidson WP, Cain NN, Sloane-Reeves JE, Giesow VE, Quijano LE and House KD (1996) 'Factors Predicting Re-referral Following Crisis Intervention for Community-based Persons with Developmental Difficulties and Behavioral and Psychiatric Disorders' *American Journal on Mental Retardation* 101 (2)

C14
Twemlow S, Fonagy P, Sacco F, Gies M, Evans R and Ewbank R (2001) 'Creating a Peaceful School Learning Environment: A controlled study of an elementary school intervention to reduce violence' *American Journal of Psychiatry* 158 (5)

C15
Webster-Stratton C (1998) 'Preventing Conduct Problems in Head Start Children: Strengthening parenting competencies' *Journal of Consulting and Clinical Psychology* 66

D Policy and official publications

D1
Barnes D, Wistow R, Dean R, Appleby C, Glover G and Bradley S (2004) *National CAMHS Mapping Exercise 2004: A summary of national trends.* London: Department of Health

D2
Department for Education and Skills (2001) *Promoting Children's Mental Health Within Early Years and School Settings.* London: Department for Education and Skills

D3
Department for Education and Skills (2004) *Removing barriers to Achievement: The Government's strategy for SEN.* Online version available at www.teachernet.gov.uk/wholeschool/sen/senstrategy (checked 5 December 2006)

D4
Department for Education and Skills (2004) *Every Child Matters: Change for children.* London: Department for Education and Skills

D5
Department for Education and Skills (2005) *Statistics of Education: Children looked after by local authorities, year ending 31/3/05 Vol I - national tables.* London: Department for Education and Skills

D6
Department of Health (2001) *Valuing People: A new strategy for learning disability for the 21st Century.* London: Department of Health

D7
Department of Health and Department for Education and Skills (2004) *The National Service Framework for Children, Young People and Maternity Services.* London: Department of Health

D8
Health Advisory Service (1986) *Bridges Over Troubled Waters, A Report from the NHS Health Advisory Service on Services for Disturbed Adolescents.* London: HMSO

D9
Health Development Agency (2004). *Promoting Emotional Health and Well-Being through the National Healthy School Standard.* Wetherby, Yorks: Health Development Agency

D10
Home Office (2006) *Give Respect, Get Respect: The Government's Respect Action Plan.* London: Home Office

D11
NHS Executive (1998) *Signposts for Success in Commissioning and Providing Health Services for People with Learning Disabilities.* London: TSO

D12
Office for Standards in Education (OFSTED) (1996) *Exclusions from Secondary Schools 1995/6.* London: HMSO

D13
Office for Standards in Education (OFSTED) (2001) *Improving Attendance and Behaviour in Secondary Schools: Strategies to promote educational inclusion.* London, OFSTED. Available online at www.ofsted.gov.uk (checked 5 December 2006)

D14
Sinclair I (2005) *Fostering Now: Messages from research.* London: Department for Education and Skills

D15
Social Exclusion Unit (1998) *Truancy and School Exclusion.* London: The Stationery Office

D16
Social Exclusion Unit & The Who Cares? Trust (2002) *Report on Education of Children and Young People in Care.* London: Social Exclusion Unit

D17
Ward H (1995) *Looking After Children: Research into practice.* London: The Stationery Office

O Other

O1
American Psychiatric Association (1994) *Diagnostic and Statistical Manual of Mental Disorders (DSM-IV).* Washington: American Psychiatric Association

O2
The Child Psychotherapy Trust (2002) *An Infant Mental Health Service: The importance of the early years and evidence-based practice.* Online version at www.childpsychotherapytrust.org.uk/pdfs/CPT_IMH_report.pdf (checked 5 December 2006)

O3
Goodman R (1997) *Child and Adolescent Mental Health Services: Reasoned advice to commissioners and providers. Maudsley Discussion Paper No 4.* London: Institute of Psychiatry

04
Morgan S (1999) *A Joint Training Curriculum for Supporting Children in Public Care*. London: National Children's Bureau

05
Rutter M and Rutter M (1993) *Developing Minds: Challenge and continuity across the life span*. London: Penguin Books.

06
Warnock M (2005) *Special Educational Needs: A new look. Impact No. 11*. London: The Philosophy of Education Society of Great Britain

07
World Health Organisation (1992) *The ICD-10 Classification of Mental and Behavioural Disorders: Clinical Descriptions and Diagnostic Guidelines*. Geneva: WHO

references - alphabetical

Alexander J, Barton C and Deal G (2005) 'Functional Family Therapy' in *Blueprints for Violence Prevention, Book 3*. Boulder, CO: Centre for the Study and Prevention of Violence A

American Psychiatric Association (1994) *Diagnostic and Statistical Manual of Mental Disorders (DSM-IV)*. Washington: American Psychiatric Association O

Armbruster P and Kazdin AE (1994) 'Attrition in Child Psychotherapy' *Advances in Clinical Child Psychology* 16 C

Audit Commission (1996) *Misspent Youth*. London: Audit Commission B

Bagley C and Pritchard (1998) 'The Reduction of Problem Behaviours and School Exclusions in at-risk Youth: An experimental study of school social work with cost benefit analysis'. *Child and Family Social Work* 3 B

Bailey S (2000) 'Serious Antisocial Behaviour' in Aggleton P, Hurry J and Warwick I (eds) *Young People and Mental Health*. Chichester: John Wiley and Sons A

Ball M (2002) *Intervening Early*. London: Department for Education and Skills B

Barlow J and Parsons J (2003) 'Group Based Parent-training Programmes for Improving Emotional and Behavioural Adjustment in 0-3 Year Old Children' *The Cochrane Database of Systematic Reviews* (2) CD003680 Oxford: Update Software A

Barlow J (1997) *Systematic Review of the Effectiveness of Parent-training Programmes in Improving Behavioural Problems in Children Aged 3-10 Years: A review of the literature on parent-training programmes and child behaviour outcome measures.* Oxford: Update Software A

Barnes D, Wistow R, Dean R, Appleby C, Glover G and Bradley S (2004) *National CAMHS Mapping Exercise 2004: A summary of national trends.* London: Department of Health D

Benson BA and Havercamp SM (2004) 'Behavioural Approaches to Treatment: Principles and practices' in Bouras N (ed), *Psychiatric and Behavioural Disorders in Developmental Disabilities and Mental Retardation.* Cambridge: Cambridge University Press A

Brady L, Harwin J, Pugh G, Scott J and Sinclair R (2005) *Specialist Fostering for Young People with Challenging Behaviour.* London: Coram Family B

Brinker RP, Seifer R and Sameroff AJ (1994) 'Relations Among Maternal Stress, Cognitive Development and Early Intervention in Middle and Low SES Infants with Developmental Disabilities' *American Journal on Mental Retardation* (4) C

Broad B (ed) (2001) *Kinship Care: The placement choice for children and young people.* Lyme Regis: Russell House B

Broad B, Hayes R and Rushforth C (2001) Kith and Kin: Kinship care for vulnerable young people. York: Joseph Rowntree Foundation/National Children's Bureau B

Brown SA, D'Amico EJ, McCarthy DM and Tapert SF (2001) 'Four-year outcomes from adolescent alcohol and drug treatment' *Journal of Studies on Alcohol* (62) 3 C

Buchanan A, Hunt J, Bretherton H and Bream V (2002) *Families in Conflict: Perspectives of children and parents on the Family Court Welfare System.* Bristol: Bristol Policy Press B

Butler I and Payne H (1997) 'The Health of Children Looked After by the Local Authority' *Adoption and Fostering* 21 B

Callaghan J, Pace F, Young B and Vostanis P (2003) 'Primary Mental Health Workers within Youth Offending Teams: A new service model' *Journal of Adolescence* 26 B

Cameron A, Lart R, Harrison L, Macdonald G and Smith R (2000) *Factors Promoting and Obstacles Hindering Joint Working: A systematic review.* Bristol: School for Policy Studies, University of Bristol A

Canning U, Millward L, Raj T and Warm D (2004) *Drug Use Prevention Among Young People: A review of reviews.* London: Health Development Agency A

Chadwick O, Taylor E and Bernard S (1998) *The Prevention of Behaviour Disorders in Children with Severe Learning Disability.* Final Report to the NHS Executive. London: Institute of Psychiatry A

Chamberlain P, Moreland S and Reid K (1992) 'Enhanced Services and Stipends for Foster Parents: Effects on retention rates and outcomes for children' *Child Welfare* 71 (5) B

Chamberlain P and Rosicky JG (1995) 'The Effectiveness of Family Therapy in the Treatment of Adolescents with Conduct Disorder and Delinquency' *Journal of Marital and Family Therapy* (21) A

Children's Mental Health Ontario (2001) *Children and Adolescents with Conduct Disorder: Findings from the literature and clinical consultation in Ontario.* Online version available at: www.cmho.org (checked 5 December 2006) A

Collishaw S, Maughan B and Goodman R (2004) 'Time trends in adolescent mental health'. *Journal of Child Psychology and Psychiatry*, 45 (8) B

Cote S, Tremblay R, Nagin D, Zoccolillo M and Vitaro F (2002) 'Childhood Behavioral Profiles Leading to Adolescent Conduct Disorder: Risk trajectories for boys and girls' *Journal of the American Academy of Child & Adolescent Psychiatry* 41 (9) C

Cotton K (1996) *School Size, School Climate and Student Performance,* School Improvement Research Series. Online version available at: www.nwrel.org/scpd/sirs/10/c020.html (checked 5 December 2006) C

Cowie H, Naylor P, Talamelli L, Chauhan P and Smith PK (2002) 'Knowledge, use of and attitudes towards peer support' *Journal of Adolescence* 25 (5) B

Deklyen M and Speltz ML (2001) 'Attachment and Conduct Disorder' in Hill J and Maughan B (eds) *Conduct Disorders in Childhood and Adolescence.* Cambridge: Cambridge University Press A

Department for Education and Skills (2001) *Promoting Children's Mental Health Within Early Years and School Settings.* London: Department for Education and Skills D

Department for Education and Skills (2004) *Removing barriers to Achievement: The Government's strategy for SEN.* Online version available at: www.teachernet.gov.uk/wholeschool/sen/senstrategy (checked September 2005) D

Department for Education and Skills (2004) *Every Child Matters: Change for children.* London: Department for Education and Skills D

Department for Education and Skills (2005) *Statistics of Education: Children looked after by local authorities, year ending 31/3/05 Vol I - national tables.* London: Department for Education and Skills

Department of Health (2001) *Valuing People: A new strategy for learning disability for the 21st Century.* London: Department of Health D

Department of Health and Department for Education and Skills (2004) *The National Service Framework for Children, Young People and Maternity Services.* London: Department of Health D

Dimigen G, Del Priore C and Butler S (1999) 'Psychiatric Disorder Among Children at Time of Entering Local Authority Care: Questionnaire survey' *British Medical Journal* 319 B

Dodge K, Dishion T and Lansford J (2006) *Deviant Peer Influences in Intervention and Public Policy for Youth.* Washington: Society for Research in Child Development. A

Dryfoos JG (1990) *Adolescents at Risk: Prevalence and prevention.* New York: Oxford University Press (USA) A

Dumaret AC, Coppel-Batsh M and Couraud S (1997) 'Adult Outcomes of Children Reared for Long Time Periods in Foster Families' *Child Abuse and Neglect* 21 B

Dunn J (2001) 'Development of Prosocial Behaviour and Conflict' in Hill J and Maughan B (eds) *Conduct Disorders in Childhood and Adolescence.* Cambridge: Cambridge University Press A

Evans J, Harden A, Thomas J and Benefield P (2003) *Support for Pupils with Emotional and Behavioural Difficulties (EBD) in Mainstream Primary School Classrooms: A systematic review of the effectiveness of interventions.* London: Evidence for Policy and Practice Information and Co-ordinating Centre (EPPI - Centre) and the National Foundation for Educational Research (NFER). A

Farrington DP (1995) 'The Development of Offending and Antisocial Behaviour from Childhood: Key findings from the Cambridge study in delinquent development' *Journal of Child Psychology and Psychiatry and Allied Disciplines* 360 B

Farrington DP (1999) 'Conduct Disorder and Deliquency' in Steinhausen HC and Verhulst FC (eds) *Risks and Outcomes in Developmental Psychopathology.* Oxford: Oxford University Press A

Ferri E and Smith K (2005) *Step Parenting in the 1990s.* London: Family Policies Studies Centre B

Flouri E (2005) *Fathering and Child Outcomes.* Chichester: Wiley A

Fonagy P and Kurtz A (2002) 'Disturbance of Conduct' in Fonagy P, Target M, Cottrell D, Phillips J and Kurtz Z (eds) *What Works for Whom? A critical review of treatments for children and adolescents.* New York: Guilford Press A

Fonagy P and Roth A (eds) (2004) *What Works For Whom? A critical review of psychotherapy research (Second Edition)* New York: Guilford Press A

Foxcroft D, Ireland D, Lister-Sharp D and Breen R (2002) 'Primary Prevention for Alcohol Misuse in Young People' The Cochrane Database of Systematic Reviews (3) A

Gardner EM (1992) 'Parent-child Interaction and Conduct Disorder' *Educational Psychology Review* 4 (2) B

Gesch CB, Hammond SM, Hampson SE, Eves A and Crowder MJ (2002) 'Influence of supplementary vitamins, minerals and essential fatty acids on the antisocial behaviour of young adult prisoners' *British Journal of Psychiatry* 181 B

Ghate D and Ramella M (2002) *A National Evaluation of the Youth Justice Board's Parenting Programme.* London: Policy Research Bureau. B

Goodman R (1997) *Child and Adolescent Mental Health Services: Reasoned advice to commissioners and providers. Maudsley Discussion Paper No 4.* London: Institute of Psychiatry O

Grella CE, Hser YI, Joshi V and Rounds-Bryant J (2001) 'Drug Treatment Outcomes for Adolescents with Co-morbid Mental and Substance Use Disorders' *The Journal of Nervous and Mental Disease* 189 C

Hallam S and Castle F (1999) *Evaluation of a School-Home Liaison Project – London Diocesan Board for Schools.* London: Institute of Education, University of London B

Hassiotis A and Hall I (2004) 'Behavioural and Cognitive-behavioural Interventions for Outwardly-directed Aggresssive Behaviour in People with Learning Disabilities' *The Cochrane Database of Systematic Reviews,* (1) A

Health Advisory Service (1986) *Bridges Over Troubled Waters, A Report from the NHS Health Advisory Service on Services for Disturbed Adolescents.* London: HMSO D

Health Development Agency (2004). *Promoting Emotional Health and Well-Being through the National Healthy School Standard.* Wetherby, Yorks: Health Development Agency D

Healy J, Gribben M and McCann C (2005) *School Restorative Conferencing. No 4 Policy and Practice Briefing.* Northern Ireland: Barnardo's. Online version available at: www.barnardos.org.uk B

Henggler S, Schoenwald S, Borduin C, Rowland MD and Cunningham PB (1998) *Multisystemic Treatment of Antisocial Behaviour in Children and Adolescents.* New York: Guilford Press A

Hill J and Maughan B (eds) (2001) *Conduct Disorders in Childhood and Adolescence.* Cambridge: Cambridge University Press A

Hinde RA (2001) 'Can the Study of "Normal" behaviour Contribute to an Understanding of Conduct Disorder?' in Hill J and Maughan B (eds) *Conduct Disorders in Childhood and Adolescence.* Cambridge: Cambridge University Press A

Holland R, Moretti MM, Verlaan V and Peterson S (1993) 'Attachment and Conduct Disorder: The Response Programme' *Canadian Journal of Psychiatry* 38 C

Home Office (2006) *Give Respect, Get Respect: The Government's Respect Action Plan.* London: Home Office D

Jaffee SR and Caspi A (2001) 'Predicting Early Fatherhood and Whether Young Fathers Live with their Children' *Journal of Child Psychology and Psychiatry*, 42 (6) B

Kazdin AE (1997) 'Practitioner Review: Psychological treatments for conduct disorder in children' *Journal of Child Psychology and Psychiatry* 38 (2) A

Kearney P, Levin E and Rosen G (2000) *Alcohol, Drug and Mental Health Problems: Working with families.* London: National Institute of Social Work B

Keenan K, Loeber R and Green S (1999) 'Conduct Disorder in Girls: A review of the literature' *Clinical Child and Family Psychology Review* 2 (1) March 1999 A

Kennedy E (2004) *Child and Adolescent Psychotherapy: A systematic review of psychoanalytic approaches.* London: North Central London Strategic Health Authority A

Liabo K (2002) 'Cognitive Behavioural Therapy for Young Offenders' *Evidence Nugget. What Works for Children?* London: City University A

Linck P, Parry-Jones B, Elliston P, Miles L and Robinson CA (2001) *The Inter-agency Working Capabilities of Local Health Groups.* Bangor: Institute of Medical and Social Care Research, University of Wales A

Littell JH, Popa M and Forsythe B (2005) 'Multisystemic Therapy for social, emotional, and behavioral problems in youth aged 10-17' *The Cochrane Database of Systematic Reviews* (4) CD004797. DOI: 10.1002/14651858.CD004797.pub4 A

Lloyd G, Stead J and Kendrick A (2001) *Hanging on in There: A study of interagency work to prevent school exclusion in three local authorities.* London: National Children's Bureau B

Lloyd N, O'Brien M and Lewis C (2003) *Fathers in Sure Start Local Programmes.* Nottingham: DfES Publications B

Loeber R and Coie J (2001) 'Continuities and Discontinuities of Development, with Particular Emphasis on Emotional and Cognitive Components of Disruptive Behaviour' in Hill J and Maughan B (eds) *Conduct Disorders in Childhood and Adolescence.* Cambridge: Cambridge University Press A

Lyne P, Allen D and Satherley P (2001) *Systematic Review of Evidence of Effective Methods for Removing Barriers to Change to Improve Collaborative Working.* Bangor: Institute for Medical and Social Care Research, University of Wales Bangor A

McCabe K, Lansing A, Garland A and Hough R (2002) 'Gender Differences in Psychopathology, Functional Impairment, and Familial Risk Factors Among Adjudicated Delinquents' *Journal of American Academy of Child and Adolescent Psychiatry* 41 C

McCann JB, James A and Wilson S (1996) 'Prevalence of Psychiatric Disorders in Young People in the Care System' *British Medical Journal* 313 B

Meltzer H, Green H, McGinnity A, Ford T and Goodman R (2005) *Mental Health of Children and Young People in Great Britain, 2004.* London: Office for National Statistics B

The Mental Health Foundation (2004) *Effective Joint Working Between CAMHS and Schools*. Research Report 412. London: Department for Education and Skills B

Moffitt TE (2003) 'Life-course-persistent and Adolescent-limited Antisocial Behavior' in Lahey B, Moffitt T and Caspi A (eds) *Causes of Conduct Disorder and Juvenile Delinquency*. New York: The Guildford Press C

Moffitt T, Caspi A, Rutter M and Silva P (2001) *Sex Differences in Antisocial Behaviour: Conduct disorder, delinquency and violence in the Dunedin longitudinal study*. Cambridge: Cambridge University Press C

Molgaard VK, Spoth RL and Redmond C (2000) *Competency Training: The strengthening families program for parents and youth 10-14*. Washington DC: Office of Juvenile Justice and Deliquency Prevention C

Montgomery P, Bjornstad G and Dennis J (2006) 'Media-based behavioural treatments for behavioural problems in children' *The Cochrane Database of Systematic Reviews* (1) CD002206. DOI: 10.1002/14651858.CD002206.pub3. A

Morgan S (1999) *A Joint Training Curriculum for Supporting Children in Public Care*. London: National Children's Bureau O

Mytton JA, Di Guiseppi C, Gough DA, Taylor R and Logan S (2002) 'School-based Violence Prevention Programmes: Systematic review of secondary prevention trials.' *Archives of Pediatrics and Adolescent Medicine* 156 A

National Institute for Health and Clinical Excellence (2006) *Parent-training/education Programmes in the Management of Children with Conduct Disorders*. London: NICE. Online version available at: www.nice.org.uk/page.aspx?o=TA102 A (checked 5 December 2006)

NHS Executive (1998) *Signposts for Success in Commissioning and Providing Health Services for People with Learning Disabilities*. London: TSO D

Oeklyen M and Speltz ML (2001) 'Attachment and conduct disorder' in Hill J and Maughan B (eds) *Conduct Disorders in Childhood and Adolescence*. Cambridge: Cambridge University Press. A

Office for Standards in Education (OFSTED) (1996) *Exclusions from Secondary Schools 1995/6*. London: HMSO D

Office for Standards in Education (OFSTED) (2001) *Improving Attendance and Behaviour in Secondary Schools: Strategies to promote educational inclusion*. London: OFSTED. Available online at: www.ofsted.gov.uk D

Offord D and Bennett K (1994) 'Conduct Disorder: Long term outcomes and intervention effectiveness' *Journal of the American Academy of Child and Adolescent Psychiatry* 33 A

Osler A, Street C, Lall M and Vincent K (2001) *Not a Problem? Girls and exclusion from school*. London: National Children's Bureau/Joseph Rowntree Foundation. B

Phillips J (1997) 'Meeting the Psychiatric Needs of Children in Foster Care: Social workers' views' *Psychiatric Bulletin* 21 B

The Prince's Trust (2002) *The Way It Is: Young people on race, school exclusion and leaving care*. London: The Prince's Trust B

Pringle A (2004) 'Can Watching Football be a Component of Developing a State of Mental Health for Men?' *The Journal of the Royal Society for the Promotion of Health*, May 2004, 124 (3) B

Quinn J (1995) 'Positive Effects of Participations in Youth Organizations' in Rutter M (ed) *Psychological Disturbances in Young People: Challenges for prevention.* Cambridge, New York, Melbourne: Cambridge University Press C

Quinton D (2004) *Supporting Parents: Messages from research.* London: Jessica Kingsley A

Qureshi H (1993) 'Impact on Families: Young adults with learning disability who show challenging behaviour' in Kleinan C (ed) *Research to Practice? Implications of research on the challenging behaviour of people with learning disability.* Kidderminster: BILD A

Reese RM, Hellings JA and Schroeder SR (2004) 'Treatment Methods for Destructive and Aggressive Behaviour in People with Severe Mental Retardation/Developmental Disabilities' in Bouras N (ed) *Psychiatric and Behavioural Disorders in Developmental Disabilities and Mental Retardation.* Cambridge: Cambridge University Press A

Richardson J (2002) *The Mental Health of Looked After Children.* London: The Mental Health Foundation. A

Richardson J and Joughin C (2002a) *Parent Training Programmes for the Management of Young Children with Conduct Disorder.* London: Gaskell A

Richardson J and Joughin C (2002b) *The Mental Health Needs of Looked After Children.* London: Gaskell. A

Richardson J and Lelliott P (2003) 'Mental Health of Looked After Children' *Advances in Psychiatric Treatment* 9 A

Roberts H, Liabo K, Lucas P, DuBois D and Sheldon T (2004) 'Mentoring to reduce antisocial behaviour in childhood' *British Medical Journal* 328 28 February. A

Rutter M (1999) 'Resilience Concepts and Findings: Implications for family therapy' *Journal of Family Therapy* 21 A

Rutter M and Rutter M (1993) *Developing Minds: Challenge and continuity across the life span.* London: Penguin Books. O

Rutter M, Giller A and Hagell A (1998) *Antisocial Behaviour by Young People.* Cambridge: Cambridge University Press A

St. James-Roberts I, Greenlaw G, Simon A and Hurry J (2005) *National Evaluation of Youth Justice Board Mentoring Schemes 2001-2004.* London: Youth Justice Board B

Sanders M, Gooley S and Nicholson J (2000) 'Early Intervention in Conduct Problems in Children' in Kosky R, O'Hanlon A, Martin G and Davis C (eds) *Clinical Approaches to Early Interventions in Child and Adolescent Mental Health (3)* Adelaide: The Australian Early Intervention Network for Mental Health in Young People A

Scott S (2004) 'Parent Training Programmes' in Rutter M and Taylor E (eds) *Child and Adolescent Psychiatry.* Oxford: Blackwell Science B

Sebba J and Sachdvev D (1997) *What Works in Inclusive Education*. Barkingside: Barnardo's A

Sellick C and Howell D (2003) *Innovative, Tried and Tested: A review of good practice in fostering. Knowledge Review 4*. London: Social Care Institute for Excellence A

Shoham VI, Davidson WP, Cain NN, Sloane-Reeves JE, Giesow VE, Quijano LE and House KD (1996) 'Factors Predicting Re-referral Following Crisis Intervention for Community-based Persons with Developmental Difficulties and Behavioral and Psychiatric Disorders' *American Journal on Mental Retardation* 101 (2) C

Sinclair I (2005) *Fostering Now: Messages from research*. London: Department for Education and Skills D

Social Exclusion Unit (1998) *Truancy and School Exclusion*. London: The Stationery Office B, D

Social Exclusion Unit and The Who Cares? Trust (2002) *Report on Education of Children and Young People in Care*. London: Social Exclusion Unit B, D

Stewart-Brown S, Fletcher L, Wadsworth M and Shaw R (2002) *The Roots of Social Capital II: A systematic review of longitudinal studies linking relationships in the home with health and disease*. Oxford: Health Services Research Unit, University of Oxford A

The Child Psychotherapy Trust (2002) *An Infant Mental Health Service: The importance of the early years and evidence-based practice*. Online version available at: www.childpsychotherapytrust.org.uk/pdfs/CPT_IMH_report.pdf (checked 5 December 2006) O

Tonge B (2004) 'Psychopathology of Children with Developmental Disabilities' in Bouras N *Psychiatric and Behavioural Disorders in Developmental Disabilities and Mental Retardation*. Cambridge: Cambridge University Press. A

Twemlow S, Fonagy P, Sacco F, Gies M, Evans R and Ewbank R (2001) 'Creating a Peaceful School Learning Environment: A controlled study of an elementary school intervention to reduce violence' *American Journal of Psychiatry* 158 (5) C

Turner W, Macdonald GM and Dennis JA (2005) 'Cognitive Behavioural Training Interventions for Assisting Foster Carers in the Management of Difficult Behaviour' in *The Cochrane Database of Systematic Reviews* 2. Oxford: Update Software A

Vernon J and Sinclair R (1998) *Maintaining Children in School: The contribution of social service departments*. London: National Children's Bureau B

Waller S, Naidoo B and Thom B (2002) *The Prevention and Reduction of Alcohol Misuse*. London: Health Development Agency A

Ward H (1995) *Looking After Children: Research into practice*. London: The Stationery Office B, D

Warnock M (2005) *Special Educational Needs: A new look. Impact No. 11*. London: The Philosophy of Education Society of Great Britain O

Webster-Stratton C (1998) 'Preventing Conduct Problems in Head Start Children: Strengthening parenting competencies' *Journal of Consulting and Clinical Psychology* 66 C

Welsh E, Buchanan A, Flouri E and Lewis J (2005) 'Involved' Fathering and Child Well-being: Fathers' involvement with secondary school children. London: National Children's Bureau B

Wilson K, Sinclair I, Taylor C, Pithouse A and Sellick C (2004) Fostering Success: An exploration of the research literature in foster care. Knowledge Review 5. London: Social Care Institute for Excellence A

Wilson SJ and Lipsey MW (2006) School-based Social Information Processing Interventions and Aggressive Behaviour for Universal Programmes (Part 1). Campbell Collaboration systematic review. Available online at: www.campbellcollaboration.org A

Wilson SJ, Lipsey MW and Derzon JH (2002) 'The Effects of School-based Intervention Programs on Aggressive and Disruptive Behaviour: A meta-analysis' Journal of Consulting and Clinical Psychology A

Wolpert M, Fuggle P and Cottrell D (2002) Drawing on the Evidence. Leicester: The British Psychological Society A

Woolfenden SR, Williams K and Peat J (2001) 'Family and Parenting Interventions in Children and Adolescents with Conduct Disorder and Delinquency Aged 10-17' in The Cochrane Database of Systematic Reviews Oxford: Update Software A

World Health Organisation (1992) The ICD-10 Classification of Mental and Behavioural Disorders: Clinical Descriptions and Diagnostic Guidelines. Geneva: WHO O

index

about the authors

Carol Joughin is a health policy and research consultant and co-author of numerous publications on health research topics including child and adolescent mental health, parent training programmes for young children with conduct disorder, attention deficit hyperactivity disorder (ADHD) and the mental health needs of looked after children. Carol has a nursing background and a master's degree in Health Management. She was heavily involved in the development of the *National Service Framework for Children, Young People and Maternity Services* (Department of Health, 2004), and prior to this was a Senior Research Fellow in the Child Health Research and Policy Unit at City University, London. She took up this research post after five years as Project Manager for the FOCUS project (1997-2002).

Dinah Morley is a consultant in child and adolescent mental health policy and development. She was Deputy Director of YoungMinds from 1997 to 2005 and has more than 20 years' experience in social care, research, teaching and the voluntary sector. She assisted in setting up the joint YoungMinds and City University MSc in child and adolescent mental health and has sat on a number of government advisory boards.

research in practice is a Department of The Dartington Hall Trust, a registered charity. Company no. 1485560 Charity no. 297756.
This paper is produced with 100% Elemental Chlorine Free pulp and is fully recyclable. It is manufactured from 50% post-consumer recycled fibre.

about research in practice

research in practice is a department of The Dartington Hall Trust run in collaboration with the University of Sheffield, the Association of Directors of Children's Services and our network of more than 100 participating agencies and consortia in England and Wales.

Our mission is to promote positive outcomes for children and families through proper and greater use of research evidence. Our services are designed to improve access to research and strengthen its understanding and adoption through the promotion of evidence-informed practice.

Keep in touch with what's going on in the research in practice network by:
- signing up on our website homepage for our monthly 'What's New' email
- asking to be put on our mailing list for our quarterly newsletter *NetWork*.

You can order or get more information about research in practice publications on our website: www.rip.org.uk/publications or by contacting our Dartington office to place an order or request a catalogue:

Blacklers, Park Road, Dartington, Totnes TQ9 6EQ
t: 01803 867692 f: 01803 868816 e: ask@rip.org.uk
www.rip.org.uk

contributing to a sustainable future for children and families

research in practice aims to improve outcomes for vulnerable children and families in England and Wales by promoting and facilitating evidence-informed practice. To recognise our role as members of the wider global community, we will donate 25% of the sale of this book and our other publications to a designated international charitable project to support a sustainable future for children and families in need. Details of the project identified for support each year are on our website: www.rip.org.uk/charity